AF553075

This Journal Belongs To

____

Please contact

____

if found

Published 2026

An Imprint of **FiNGERPRINT!**
Prakash Books

www.whitearrowbooks.com

This journal is intended as a supportive tool for reflection and growth. It is not a substitute for professional medical advice, therapy or support groups.

ISBN: 9789370894242

This journal is a companion. It is not here to diagnose you or demand anything of you. It is here to walk beside you as you navigate your journey of sobriety, using a tool that has endured for over two thousand years: the principles of Stoic philosophy.

At the heart of Stoicism lies a powerful, liberating idea: "We do not control what happens to us—but we always control how we respond." This is the bedrock of resilience, and for those who choose sobriety—whether as a path to clarity, discipline or self-respect—this truth becomes a daily compass.

When life feels overwhelming or unpredictable, the Stoics remind us: Return to what you can control. Return to your own mind. Choosing this path is not a retreat, it is an act of courage.

There may be days when you step away, and that's expected. Toward the end of the journal, however, you'll find a place to begin again, as many times as you need.

Each daily entry in this journal offers a reflection, rooted in the wisdom of thinkers like Marcus Aurelius, Epictetus and Seneca. Their ideas have been translated into simple, grounded practices you can apply directly to your day by observing your thoughts, anchoring your emotions and taking responsibility for your choices.

Remember, the goal isn't to master anything overnight but to build something gradually with small, steady reminders of who you are and who you're becoming.

You don't need to be familiar with Stoicism to use this journal. All you need is a willingness to be honest with yourself, one page at a time. Some days, the words may resonate deeply; other days, they may challenge you. That's okay. Growth doesn't always feel comfortable but it is always worth it.

Your future begins now, with a pen in your hand and your attention to what truly matters.

So, take a deep breath. Begin where you are. And turn the page.

DAY 1

"The happiness of your life depends upon the quality of your thoughts." MARCUS AURELIUS

Marcus Aurelius, the Roman emperor and Stoic philosopher, understood that true power lies in controlling our minds. In recovery, we often struggle with negative thoughts and self-doubt. Stoicism teaches us to examine those thoughts, challenge their validity and choose more empowering perspectives. By focusing on what we can control—our thoughts and actions—we break free from the cycle of addiction and build a foundation for lasting happiness.

COGNITIVE REFRAMING

Identify a recurring negative thought related to your sobriety (e.g., "I'm not strong enough," "I'll never be truly happy sober").

Challenge This Thought by Asking: Is this thought 100 percent true? Is there another way to look at this situation? What evidence supports this thought, and what evidence contradicts it?

Reframe the negative thought into a more empowering statement (e.g., I am making progress every day. Sobriety allows me to experience authentic joy).

Repeat this affirmation throughout the day whenever the recurring negative thought arises.

I am worthy of happy thoughts and a happy life.

DAY 2

"There is only one way to happiness and that is to cease worrying about things which are beyond the power of our will." EPICTETUS

Epictetus reminds us of the futility of dwelling on things we cannot control. In recovery, we may fixate on past mistakes, the actions of others or future fears. Stoicism encourages us to accept what is, focus our energy on our own choices and find peace in the present moment. Letting go of external anxieties allows us to embrace the journey of sobriety with clarity and strength.

LETTING GO OF WHAT CANNOT BE CONTROLLED

Identify Sources of Worry: Write down everything that worries you throughout the day.

Examine Their Circumstances: Divide this list into two parts—causes of worry that can be alleviated by your actions and causes that are independent of your actions.

Define Your Priorities: Take a look at the causes of worry your actions can alleviate. Write down small steps to work through these problems.

I will focus on what I can control, and I will accept what I cannot.

DAY 3

"When force of circumstance upsets your equanimity, lose no time in recovering your self-control, and do not remain out of tune longer than you can help."
MARCUS AURELIUS

Sobriety is not always easy. We face setbacks, cravings and difficult emotions. Marcus Aurelius, the Stoic philosopher, recognized that challenges are opportunities for growth. Each obstacle we overcome in recovery builds our mental strength, resilience and determination. Embracing the difficulties, rather than fearing them, allows us to transform our struggles into sources of personal power.

OBSTACLES ARE THE WAY

Recall a recent challenge you faced in your sobriety journey.

Instead of viewing it as a failure, ask yourself—

- What can I learn from this?
- How can this experience make me stronger?
- What positive actions can I take as a result of this obstacle?

Write down three specific actions you can take to turn this obstacle into an opportunity for growth.

I welcome setbacks as I believe in my strength to overcome them.

DAY 4

"Waste no more time arguing what a good man should be. Be one." MARCUS AURELIUS

In recovery, we often strive to be our "best selves," but this can feel like an overwhelming goal. Marcus Aurelius encourages us to stop overthinking and simply act with integrity, kindness and courage. Choosing sobriety is an act of becoming a better person. Every day we choose to live in accordance with our values, we are embodying the essence of a "good man" (or woman).

ACTS OF VIRTUE

Identify three small but meaningful acts of virtue you can perform today. These could be:

- Acts of kindness toward others.
- Acts of self-care that support your sobriety.
- Acts of courage in facing challenging situations.

Write these down and commit to performing them today. Remember, true virtue is expressed through action, not just intention.

The person I want to be is ________, ________ and ________. My sobriety is helping me become that person.

DAY 5

"God grant me the serenity to accept the things I cannot change, courage to change the things I can, and the wisdom to know the difference." REINHOLD NIEBUHR

The above prayer, though not directly attributed to the Stoics, resonates deeply with their philosophy. It acknowledges the fundamental Stoic principle of dichotomy—the division between what we can and cannot control. In recovery, this distinction is paramount. We cannot control the past, the actions of others or the initial urge to reach for a drink or a drug. But we can control our reactions, our choices, our commitment to sobriety in this very moment.

DICHOTOMY OF CONTROL

Identify Your Struggle: What is a current source of anxiety or frustration in your recovery? Write it down.

Analyze and Divide: Carefully consider this struggle. Break it down into two columns.

- *Things I can control:* My reactions, my actions, my commitment to staying sober, seeking support.
- *Things I cannot control:* Other people's opinions, cravings, the past.

Shift Your Focus: Consciously shift your energy and attention to the "can control" column. What specific actions can you take today to address the elements within your control?

I am not defined by the opinions of others. I choose to define myself through my commitment to sobriety and personal growth.

DAY 6

"The impediment to action advances action. What stands in the way becomes the way."
MARCUS AURELIUS

Aurelius, even as emperor of Rome, recognized that life is full of obstacles. We, on the path to sobriety, encounter our own unique set of challenges—cravings, triggers, social pressures and the lingering weight of past mistakes. Yet, Stoicism teaches us to view these obstacles not as roadblocks but as opportunities for cultivating virtue.

TURNING OBSTACLES INTO OPPORTUNITIES

Acknowledge Your Obstacle: Identify a recent challenge or setback you've faced in your recovery journey.

Embrace the Struggle: Resist the urge to become discouraged or defeated. Instead, view this obstacle as a test of your resilience.

Seek the Lesson: Ask yourself—
- What can I learn from this experience?
- How can this challenge make me stronger and more resilient?
- What tools or support systems can I utilize to overcome this?

Take Action: Identify three specific actions you can take to turn this obstacle into an opportunity for growth.

Every challenge I overcome strengthens my resolve and brings me closer to my goal of lasting sobriety.

DAY 7

"Don't seek for everything to happen as you wish it would, but rather wish that everything happens as it actually will—then your life will flow well." EPICTETUS

Epictetus, born a slave, understood the importance of acceptance. In recovery, we often struggle with wishing things were different, wishing we hadn't made past mistakes, wishing cravings would disappear, wishing the road to sobriety was always smooth. This resistance to reality only breeds suffering. The Stoic concept of *amor fati,* or "love of fate," encourages us to accept what is, rather than fight against it.

PRACTICING AMOR FATI

Identify Your Resistance: What aspect of your recovery journey are you currently resisting? Write it down.

Acknowledge What Is: Take a deep breath and acknowledge that this is your current reality. Resisting it will not make it disappear.

Shift Your Perspective: Instead of focusing on how you wish things were different, ask yourself—

- What can I learn from this situation?
- How can I find acceptance and even gratitude within this moment?
- What opportunities for growth or positive action exist within this reality?

I embrace my reality with courage and acceptance, finding gratitude in each step of my journey.

DAY 8

"The greatest weapon against stress is our ability to choose one thought over another." WILLIAM JAMES

In recovery, our inner critic—that voice of self-doubt and negativity—can be a powerful trigger, leading to feelings of unworthiness and fueling the urge to relapse. Taming this inner critic is crucial for maintaining sobriety.

QUIETING THE INNER CRITIC

Identify the Negative Thought: Pay attention to your self-talk. What negative thoughts or beliefs about yourself frequently surface, especially in relation to your sobriety? Write them down.

Challenge the Thought: Don't just accept these thoughts as truth. Challenge them by asking—

- Is this thought 100 percent true?
- What evidence supports this thought, and what evidence contradicts it?

Reframe with Positive Affirmations: Replace those negative thoughts with positive, empowering statements. For example—

- Instead of "I'm not strong enough," affirm, "I am choosing strength every day."
- Instead of "I'm a failure," affirm, "I am a work in progress, capable of growth and change."

I am worthy of recovery; I am capable of change, and I choose to focus on positive self-beliefs.

DAY 9

"Let us prepare our minds as if we'd come to the very end of life. Let us postpone nothing. Let us balance life's books each day... The one who puts the finishing touches on their life each day is never short of time." SENECA

The Stoic practice of *memento mori*—meditating on death—may seem morbid, but it's actually a powerful tool for living a more fulfilling life. Recognizing our own mortality reminds us of the preciousness of time and the importance of aligning our actions with our values. This is especially poignant in recovery, where each day is a gift.

MEMENTO MORI

Find a Quiet Space: Sit or lie down in a comfortable position. Close your eyes and take a few deep breaths.

Contemplate Your Mortality: Gently bring to mind the reality that your time on this earth is finite. Reflect on the fact that one day, you will no longer be here.

Embrace Gratitude: Instead of fear or sadness, allow this awareness to cultivate a sense of gratitude for the present moment. What are you grateful for in your life right now?

Live with Intention: Ask yourself—

- Knowing that my time is limited, how do I want to spend the rest of my life?
- How can I align my actions with my values, starting today?

I am grateful for the gift of this day, and I choose to live it with intention, courage and purpose.

DAY 10

"Progress is not achieved by luck or accident but by working on yourself daily." EPICTETUS

Recovery is a journey, not a destination. Epictetus reminds us that a lasting change requires consistent effort, day after day. There are no shortcuts to sobriety. It's built upon the foundation of daily choices, small victories and a relentless commitment to personal growth.

DAILY MORAL INVENTORY

Review Your Actions: Reflect on your choices and behaviors throughout the day.

- Where did I demonstrate strength and commitment to my sobriety?
- Where did I struggle or face challenges?

Acknowledge and Learn:

- Celebrate your successes, no matter how small.
- Identify any triggers or situations that led to difficulty. What can you learn from them?
- How can you approach similar situations differently in the future?

Set an Intention: Choose one specific action you will focus on tomorrow to further strengthen your sobriety.

Every day is a new opportunity to make choices that support my sobriety and well-being.

DAY 11

"The best revenge is to be unlike him who performed the injury." MARCUS AURELIUS

In recovery, we may grapple with anger and resentment toward those who have hurt us, perhaps even contributing to our addiction. Aurelius offers a powerful alternative to vengeance: rising above the behavior of those who have wronged us. True strength lies in choosing a different path—the path of healing, forgiveness and personal growth.

RELEASING RESENTMENT

Holding on to anger and resentment is like drinking poison and expecting the other person to die. It harms us far more than it harms them. Practice releasing these toxic emotions.

Acknowledge the Hurt: Allow yourself to feel the pain and anger you've been carrying. Suppression only strengthens these emotions.

Choose to Forgive: Forgiveness doesn't condone the actions of others; it frees you from the grip of their past behavior.

Focus on Your Growth: Shift your energy toward your own healing and well-being. How can you use this experience as a catalyst for personal growth?

I choose to release the weight of the past and embrace the freedom of forgiveness.

DAY 12

"Man is not worried by real problems so much as by his imagined anxieties about real problems." EPICTETUS

Anxiety and worry are common companions in recovery. We may fixate on potential triggers, fear judgment from others or doubt our ability to stay sober in challenging situations. Epictetus reminds us of the futility of dwelling on what we cannot control. Our energy is best spent focusing on what we *can* influence—our actions, our choices and our commitment to recovery in this present moment.

LETTING GO OF WHAT YOU CANNOT CONTROL

Identify Your Worries: Write down the specific things causing you anxiety related to your sobriety.

Circle What You Can Control: Are these worries within your power to change? Circle those that are.

Surrender the Rest: For those worries outside your control, practice releasing them. This might involve—

- Visualizing yourself letting go of a balloon filled with your anxieties.
- Repeating a calming mantra, such as, "I release what I cannot control."

I choose to focus on what I can control—my actions, my thoughts, my recovery—and release the worry I have over things beyond my influence.

DAY 13

Enjoy present pleasures in such a way as not to injure future ones." SENECA

In the past, our pursuit of pleasure may have been driven by our desire for instant gratification—the quick fix, the fleeting high, the temporary escape from discomfort. Seneca reminds us to approach pleasure with a long-term perspective, considering the consequences of our actions. True, sustainable pleasure in recovery comes from aligning our choices with our values and building a life that brings genuine fulfillment.

CHOOSING SUSTAINABLE PLEASURE

Reflect on Past Patterns: What types of pleasure-seeking behaviors were harmful in your past? How did those choices ultimately lead to pain or negative consequences?

Identify Values-Aligned Pleasures: What brings you genuine joy and satisfaction that is also aligned with your commitment to sobriety and well-being? This might include—

- Connecting with loved ones.
- Engaging in creative pursuits.

Make Conscious Choices: Each day, prioritize activities that bring you sustainable pleasure, knowing that these choices contribute to your long-term happiness and well-being.

I choose to engage in activities that bring me genuine pleasure, knowing that true happiness comes from living in alignment with my values.

DAY 14

"The tranquility that comes when you stop caring what they say. Or think, or do. Only what you do."
MARCUS AURELIUS

We often seek validation and happiness from external sources—approval from others, material possessions, fleeting highs. Aurelius reminds us that true happiness is an inside job. It comes from living in accordance with our values, cultivating inner peace and finding contentment in the present moment, regardless of external circumstances.

CULTIVATING INTERNAL VALIDATION

Identify External Sources of Validation: What do you seek validation from outside yourself? This might be—

- Likes on social media platforms.
- Achievements or status.

Shift Your Focus Inward: Instead of seeking external validation, focus on cultivating the following qualities within yourself—

- Self-compassion.
- Self-acceptance.
- Gratitude for your strengths and accomplishments.

Practice Self-Celebration: Acknowledge and celebrate your wins, no matter how small. Recognize the progress you're making on your sobriety journey.

My worth comes from within. I am enough, just as I am.

DAY 15

"Waste no more time arguing what a good man should be. Be one." MARCUS AURELIUS

It's easy to get caught up in the "shoulds" of recovery—what we *should* be doing, how we *should* be feeling, who we *should* be. Aurelius cuts through the noise, reminding us that true transformation comes from action, not endless contemplation. Remember, each day is an opportunity to embody the values of sobriety—honesty, courage, kindness, resilience.

ALIGNING ACTIONS WITH YOUR VALUES

Define Your Values: What qualities are important to you in your recovery journey? Some examples might include honesty, integrity, self-respect, compassion and perseverance.

Identify Opportunities for Action: As you go through your day, look for small but meaningful ways to live in accordance with these values. This might be—

- Speaking kindly to yourself and others.
- Showing up for a commitment, even when it's challenging.
- Offering support to someone who is struggling.

I choose my actions with intention, aligning them with my values and building a life of integrity.

DAY 16

"Misfortune is virtue's opportunity." SENECA

Sobriety is not a magical cure-all. It doesn't erase life's challenges or guarantee a life free from hardship. There will be tough days, moments of weakness and unexpected obstacles. But as Seneca reminds us, these difficulties are not setbacks, they are opportunities to build resilience, develop coping skills and emerge stronger on the other side.

REFRAMING CHALLENGES FOR GROWTH

Identify a Recent Challenge: What is a difficult situation you've encountered recently in your recovery journey? Write it down.

Shift Your Perspective: Instead of viewing this as a failure or setback, ask yourself—

- What can I learn from this experience?
- How can I use this to develop my resilience and coping skills?
- What positive actions can I take in response to this challenge?

Create a Plan of Action: Write down three specific steps you can take to move forward with strength and purpose.

I embrace challenges as opportunities for growth, trusting in my ability to overcome adversity and emerge stronger.

DAY 17

"The chief task in life is simply this: to identify and separate matters so that I can say clearly to myself which are externals not under my control and which have to do with the choices I actually control." EPICTETUS

In recovery, it's easy to fall into the trap of blaming external factors for our struggles—stressful situations, difficult people, the availability of substances. Epictetus reminds us that our true power lies in recognizing what we can and cannot control. While we can't control everything that happens to us, we can control our reactions, our choices and our commitment to sobriety.

DICHOTOMY OF CONTROL

Identify a Source of Stress: What is a current situation or event in your life that is causing you stress, anxiety or temptation related to your sobriety?

Draw Two Columns: Label one column "Within My Control" and the other "Not Within My Control."

Categorize and Strategize: Carefully consider each aspect of the stressful situation. Place each element in the appropriate column.

- For those within your control, create a plan of action. What specific steps can you take to address these aspects?
- For those outside your control, practice acceptance and release.

I have the power to choose my responses, even in challenging situations. I choose sobriety.

DAY 18

"Don't explain your philosophy. Embody it."
EPICTETUS

We can easily get caught up in talking about recovery, analyzing our progress or intellectually engaging with the principles of sobriety. While self-reflection is valuable, true transformation occurs when we embody our commitment to sobriety in every action, every choice and every interaction.

LIVING YOUR SOBRIETY BEYOND WORDS

Reflect on Your Actions: Are your behaviors consistently reflecting your commitment to sobriety? Are there any areas where your actions don't align with your words?

Identify Opportunities for Embodiment: How can you more fully live your sobriety today? This might involve—

- Showing up for a support group meeting with authenticity and vulnerability.
- Setting healthy boundaries with people who don't support your recovery.

Let Your Actions Speak Louder Than Words: Focus on making choices that reflect your commitment to sobriety, allowing your actions to speak for themselves.

I am not defined by my past mistakes. I am defined by my actions today, and I choose to embody the principles of sobriety in all that I do.

DAY 19

"It never ceases to amaze me: we all love ourselves more than other people, but care more about their opinion than our own." MARCUS AURELIUS

The opinions and judgments of others can be a powerful trigger in early recovery. We may fear being judged for our past mistakes or feel the need to prove ourselves to those who doubted our ability to change. Aurelius's words remind us that true freedom comes from prioritizing our self-acceptance over the ever-shifting sands of external validation.

RELEASING THE NEED FOR EXTERNAL VALIDATION

Identify Your Fears: What are you afraid of people thinking or saying about you in relation to your sobriety? Write down these fears without judgment.

Challenge the Thoughts: Are these fears based in reality? Do the opinions of others truly dictate your worth or the validity of your recovery journey?

Focus on Your Own Approval: Remind yourself that the most important approval you need is your own. Are you proud of the progress you're making? Are you living in alignment with your values?

I am worthy of love and acceptance, starting with myself. My recovery journey is mine alone, and I choose to define my own success.

DAY 20

"The greatest remedy for anger is delay." SENECA

Anger is a powerful emotion that can easily hijack our best intentions. We may feel anger toward ourselves for past mistakes, toward others who have hurt us or even toward the challenges of sobriety itself. Seneca wisely advises us to meet anger with delay, allowing time for the initial intensity to subside before reacting.

PAUSE BEFORE REACTION

Recognize the Triggers: What situations or people tend to evoke anger or irritability in you? Become aware of your personal triggers.

Practice the Pause: When you feel anger rising, resist the urge to react immediately. Take a few deep breaths, step away from the situation if possible and create some distance between the trigger and your response.

Choose a Different Path: Once the initial surge of anger has subsided, ask yourself—

- What is a more constructive way to respond to this situation?
- How can I communicate my needs or boundaries without resorting to anger?

I choose to respond to challenging situations with patience and understanding, knowing that anger only creates more suffering.

DAY 21

"There is a time for everything and a season for every activity under the heavens." ECCLESIASTES 3:1

In recovery, we often feel a sense of urgency to "fix" everything at once—our past mistakes, our relationships, our lives. We may set unrealistic expectations, pushing ourselves too hard, too fast. This verse from Ecclesiastes reminds us that everything has its own natural rhythm and timing. There is a time for healing, a time for growth, a time for patience and a time for action.

HONORING THE NATURAL RHYTHM OF RECOVERY

Identify Areas of Impatience: Where in your recovery journey are you feeling a sense of urgency or pressure to make progress quickly? Write it down.

Practice Acceptance: Remind yourself that recovery is a process, not a race. It takes time for wounds to heal, for new habits to form, for trust to be rebuilt.

Focus on the Present: Instead of dwelling on the past or worrying about the future, bring your attention to what you can do today to nurture your sobriety. What small act of self-care, connection or service can you engage in right now?

I trust in the timing of my own journey. I am exactly where I need to be in this moment.

DAY 22

"The man who is not the master of himself is at the mercy of others." SENECA

At the heart of Stoicism lies the belief that true freedom comes not from external circumstances, but from mastering our minds and emotions. For those in recovery, this resonates deeply. Addiction often stems from a feeling of being powerless over our impulses and desires. Sobriety, then, becomes a journey of reclaiming our inner authority and learning to govern ourselves with wisdom and compassion.

CULTIVATING SELF-MASTERY

Identify Your Impulses: What are your typical reactions to stress, boredom, loneliness or anger? Become aware of the patterns that may have driven addictive behaviors in the past.

Choose a Different Response: Instead of reacting on autopilot, practice pausing, observing your impulses and making a conscious choice about how you want to respond. This might involve—

- Walking away from a triggering situation.
- Calling a supportive friend instead of reaching for a substance.
- Engaging in healthy coping mechanisms like exercising.

I am in control of my choices. I choose to respond to life's challenges with strength, wisdom and self-compassion.

DAY 23

"Associate with those who will make a better man of you. Welcome those who you yourself can improve. The process is mutual, for men learn while they teach."
SENECA

The company we keep has a profound impact on our thoughts, behaviors and overall well-being. Surrounding ourselves with people who support our recovery, inspire us to grow and hold us accountable is crucial for long-term sobriety. As Seneca reminds us, this is a two-way street—we should also strive to be a source of support and inspiration for others.

CULTIVATING A SUPPORTIVE COMMUNITY

Evaluate Your Relationships: Take an honest look at the people in your life. Do they uplift and inspire you? Do they support your sobriety? Or do they drain your energy and tempt you to fall back into old patterns?

Set Healthy Boundaries: It's okay to distance yourself from relationships that no longer serve your highest good, even if it's difficult. Your well-being and sobriety are paramount.

Seek Out Positive Influences: Actively cultivate connections with people who embody the qualities you admire—those who are kind, compassionate, supportive and committed to their own growth.

I am worthy of healthy, supportive relationships. I choose to surround myself with people who uplift and inspire me.

DAY 24

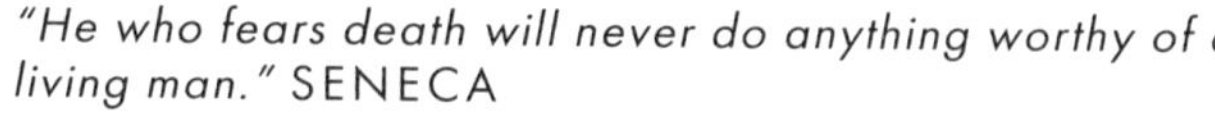

"He who fears death will never do anything worthy of a living man." SENECA

In sobriety, we often tiptoe around the fear of relapse, the fear of judgment, even the fear of success. But these fears can paralyze us. Seneca reminds us that true living requires courage—to step outside our comfort zones, to embrace risks, to live fully, knowing that setbacks and challenges are inevitable parts of growth.

FACING YOUR FEARS

Identify Your Fears: What fears are holding you back in your recovery journey? Write them down. Don't judge them; simply acknowledge their presence.

Challenge the Validity: Gently question each fear. Is it based in reality or on past experiences that may no longer apply? What is the worst-case scenario, and how likely is it to occur?

Take Small Steps: You don't have to conquer all your fears at once. Choose one fear and identify a small, manageable step you can take to face it. For example, if you fear attending social events sober, start by attending a recovery meeting with new people.

I am stronger than my fears. I choose courage over comfort, trusting in my ability to navigate challenges and create a fulfilling life in sobriety.

DAY 25

"The universe is change; our life is what our thoughts make it." MARCUS AURELIUS

We can't control everything that happens to us, but we can always choose our perspective. This fundamental Stoic principle reminds us that our thoughts have immense power. If we dwell on negative thoughts, resentments, or anxieties, we create our own suffering. But if we focus on gratitude, acceptance and positive self-talk, we pave the way for greater peace and fulfillment.

SHIFTING YOUR OUTLOOK

Notice Your Thoughts: Pay attention to your internal dialogue throughout the day. What types of thoughts dominate your mind—positive, negative, neutral? Don't judge yourself, simply observe.

Challenge Negative Thoughts: When you notice negative, self-critical or fear-based thoughts, gently challenge their validity. Ask yourself—

- Is this thought 100 percent true?
- Is there another, more balanced way to look at this situation?
- What would I say to a dear friend who was having this thought?

My thoughts create my reality. I choose to focus on thoughts that empower me, uplift me and support my recovery.

DAY 26

"We suffer more often in imagination than in reality."
SENECA

Our minds are powerful tools, but they can also be our worst enemies. We often create more suffering for ourselves through anxious anticipation, overthinking and dwelling on worst-case scenarios. Seneca reminds us that much of our anxiety stems not from actual events but from our own imagined interpretations of them.

GROUNDING YOURSELF IN THE PRESENT MOMENT

Identify Your Worry Spiral: What situations or triggers tend to send you into a spiral of worry or overthinking? Write it down.

Engage Your Senses: When you find yourself lost in anxious thoughts, bring your attention to the present moment by engaging your five senses.

- *Sight:* What do you see around you right now?
- *Sound:* What sounds can you hear?
- *Touch:* Notice the feeling of your feet on the ground.
- *Smell:* What scents do you sense in the air?
- *Taste:* Take a sip of water and notice the taste.

I choose to focus on the present moment, releasing anxieties about the future and finding peace in the here and now.

DAY 27

"The key is to keep company only with people who uplift you, whose presence calls forth your best."
EPICTETUS

The people we surround ourselves with have a profound impact on our well-being. Just as iron sharpens iron, spending time with individuals who are positive, supportive and committed to their own growth can inspire and motivate us on our own journeys. This is especially crucial in recovery, where a strong support system can mean the difference between relapse and lasting sobriety.

TAKING INVENTORY OF YOUR SOCIAL CIRCLE

Reflect on Your Relationships: Take some time to consider the people you spend the most time with.

- Do they support your sobriety?
- Do they inspire you to be a better version of yourself?

Set Healthy Boundaries: If there are people in your life who are not conducive to your recovery, it's okay to create distance, even if it's temporary.

Build Positive Connections: Look to connect with those who are positive influences in your life. Find those who embody the values you admire, whether it is kindness, compassion or honesty, and learn in their company.

I deserve to be surrounded by people who uplift and inspire me. I choose to spend my time with those who support my growth and celebrate my journey.

DAY 28

"Accept the things to which fate binds you and love the people with whom fate brings you together, but do so with all your heart." MARCUS AURELIUS

We often waste precious energy resisting reality, wishing things were different or holding on to resentment about the past. Aurelius reminds us that true peace comes from acceptance—accepting what is within our control, releasing what is not and finding joy in the present moment, even amid life's inevitable challenges.

PRACTICING ACCEPTANCE AND GRATITUDE

Identify Areas of Resistance: What are you currently resisting in your recovery journey? This might be a difficult emotion, a challenging situation or a lingering resentment.

Acknowledge What Is: Instead of fighting against reality, take a deep breath and acknowledge the truth of the situation. This doesn't mean you have to like it, simply that you choose to accept it as your current reality.

Shift Your Perspective:
Ask yourself—

- Is there anything I can learn from this situation?
- Is there any hidden opportunity within this challenge?"
- What am I grateful for in this moment, despite the difficulty?

I embrace the present moment with an open heart, finding gratitude even amid challenges and trusting in the unfolding of my own unique journey.

DAY 29

"Whoever values peace of mind and the health of the soul will live the best of all possible lives."
MARCUS AURELIUS

It is common to struggle with anger and resentment in recovery, especially toward those who might have hurt us or contributed to our addiction. However, seeking revenge or holding on to anger only perpetuates a cycle of pain. True strength lies in choosing a different path—the path of forgiveness, compassion and personal growth.

RELEASING RESENTMENT

Acknowledge the Hurt: Allow yourself to feel the pain, anger or resentment you've been carrying. Suppression only strengthens these emotions. Write it down, talk it out with a trusted friend or express it through art or journaling.

Focus on Your Growth: Instead of dwelling on the past, shift your energy toward your own healing and well-being. Ask yourself—

- What have I learned from this experience?
- How can I use this pain as a catalyst for personal growth?

Practice Compassion: Try to cultivate a sense of compassion for the person who hurt you. Recognize that they, too, are human and capable of making mistakes.

I choose to release the weight of the past and embrace the freedom of forgiveness.

DAY 30

"You have power over your mind—not outside events. Realize this, and you will find strength."
MARCUS AURELIUS

Life is full of unpredictable events, both positive and negative. We can't control the weather, the traffic, the opinions of others, or the curveballs that life throws our way. But as Aurelius wisely reminds us, we always have control over our own minds. This realization is incredibly empowering, especially in recovery, where we're often faced with triggers, temptations and challenges.

FINDING INNER STRENGTH

Identify External Factors: What are some things in your life that you often feel powerless over?

Shift Your Focus: Instead of dwelling on what you can't control, consciously choose to focus on what you *can* influence.

- *Your thoughts:* Challenge negative thinking patterns, practice gratitude and focus on positive affirmations.
- *Your actions:* Make choices that align with your values and support your recovery, even when it's difficult.
- *Your responses:* You can't control what happens to you, but you can choose your responses. Practice patience, compassion and forgiveness.

I am not defined by my circumstances. I have the power to choose my responses. I choose strength, resilience and recovery.

DAY 31

"The obstacle in the path becomes the path. Never forget, within every obstacle is an opportunity to improve our condition." RYAN HOLIDAY

We often perceive challenges as roadblocks on the path to recovery. However, Aurelius encourages us to view obstacles as opportunities for growth and learning. Each challenge we overcome, each craving we resist, each setback we navigate makes us stronger, more resilient and more deeply committed to our sobriety.

TRANSFORMING OBSTACLES INTO OPPORTUNITIES

Identify the Obstacle: What is a current challenge or obstacle you are facing in your recovery journey?

Shift Your Perspective: Instead of viewing this obstacle as a defeat, ask yourself—

- What can I learn from this experience?
- How can I use this challenge to strengthen my resolve and build resilience?
- What resources or support systems can I utilize to help me overcome this obstacle?

Create a Plan of Action: Write down three specific actions you can take to move through this challenge and come out stronger on the other side.

I embrace challenges as opportunities for growth. I am resourceful, resilient and capable of overcoming any obstacle that comes my way.

DAY 32

"If you are distressed by anything external, the pain is not due to the thing itself, but to your estimate of it; and this you have the power to revoke at any moment."
MARCUS AURELIUS

Our thoughts have incredible power to shape our experiences. It's not necessarily the external event itself that causes us suffering; rather, it is our interpretation of the event. We often add layers of judgment, criticism and worst-case scenarios that amplify our pain. Aurelius reminds us that we have the power to choose a different perspective.

CHALLENGING YOUR INTERPRETATIONS

Identify the Source of Distress: What external situation or event is causing you stress, anxiety or temptation?

Examine Your Thoughts: What are the thoughts running through your mind about this situation? Write them down without judgment.

Challenge the Validity: Are these thoughts 100 percent true? What evidence supports your thoughts, and what evidence contradicts them?

Choose a More Empowering Perspective: Can you find a more neutral, balanced or even positive way to view this situation? How would someone you admire approach this challenge?

I am not my thoughts. I have the power to choose my perspective, and I choose thoughts that empower me and support my well-being.

DAY 33

"The happiness of your life depends upon the quality of your thoughts." MARCUS AURELIUS

Our minds are powerful creators. The thoughts we habitually focus on shape our emotions, our behaviors and ultimately, our experience of life. If we dwell on negativity, self-criticism or fear, we create more suffering for ourselves. However, if we cultivate positive thoughts, gratitude and self-compassion, we pave the way for greater peace and fulfillment.

CULTIVATING POSITIVE SELF-TALK

Become Aware of Your Inner Dialogue: Pay attention to your thoughts throughout the day. What types of thoughts tend to dominate your mind—positive, negative or neutral?

Challenge Negative Thoughts: When you notice negative or self-critical thoughts, gently challenge their validity. Are they based on facts or on old patterns of thinking?

Replace with Positive Affirmations: Create a list of positive affirmations that resonate with you and support your recovery. For example—

- I am strong and capable.
- I choose sobriety each and every day.
- I am worthy of love and respect.

I choose to focus on positive thoughts. My thoughts create my reality, and I choose thoughts that empower me and support my well-being.

DAY 34

"Don't explain your philosophy. Embody it."
EPICTETUS

It's easy to get caught up in the intellectual aspects of recovery—reading books, attending meetings and discussing the principles of sobriety. While knowledge is important, true transformation occurs when we put these principles into action, embodying our commitment to sobriety in our daily choices and behaviors.

ALIGNING ACTIONS WITH YOUR VALUES

Define Your Values: What qualities are most important to you in your recovery journey? This might include—

- Honesty
- Integrity
- Courage
- Compassion
- Perseverance

Identify Opportunities for Alignment: As you go through your day, look for ways to make choices that reflect these values. This might involve—

- Showing up for your commitments, even when it's difficult.
- Choosing honesty over convenience.
- Offering support to someone who is struggling.

My actions speak louder than words. I choose to embody my values in everything I do, creating a life of integrity and purpose.

DAY 35

"Waste no more time arguing what a good man should be. Be one." MARCUS AURELIUS

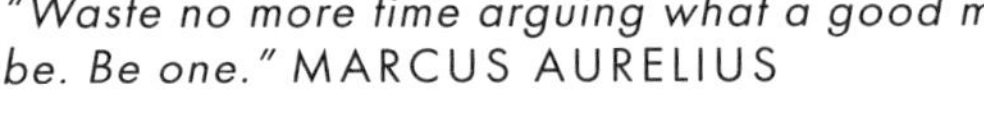

In recovery, it is easy to get caught up in what you feel you should be doing. Aurelius reminds us that endless contemplation leads nowhere—action comes first. When you find yourself asking questions, such as what you should be doing, how you should be feeling or who you should be, remind yourself of the moments in each day when you can instead embody the qualities you admire, such as kindness, courage, integrity and compassion.

LIVING YOUR VALUES, TODAY

Choose One Value: From the list of values that you identified yesterday, choose one to focus on today.

Identify Opportunities for Action: As you go through your day, look for small but meaningful ways to express this value through your actions. This might involve—

- Practicing patience with a difficult person.
- Showing up for a commitment, even if you're tired.
- Speaking up for what you believe in, even if it's uncomfortable.
- Offering a helping hand to someone in need.

I am a work in progress. I choose to focus on progress, not perfection, celebrating each step I take toward becoming the best version of myself.

DAY 36

"First say to yourself what you would be; and then do what you have to do." EPICTETUS

It's easy to get caught up in the day-to-day challenges of recovery and lose sight of the bigger picture. Epictetus reminds us to connect with our vision for the future—who we want to become, what we want to experience, how we want to feel. By clarifying our aspirations, we gain a sense of purpose and direction that can guide us through difficult moments.

CONNECTING WITH YOUR VISION

Visualize Your Ideal Self: Take a few moments to imagine yourself living a life of sobriety. Who are you with? What are you doing? How do you feel? Engage all your senses to create a vivid picture in your mind.

Identify the Qualities: What qualities define this ideal version of yourself? What strengths do you embody? What values guide your actions?

Bridge the Gap: What steps can you take today to align your actions with this vision? What choices can you make that will move you closer to becoming this person?

I am capable of creating the life I desire. I choose to focus on my goals, embrace my potential and take action toward my dreams.

DAY 37

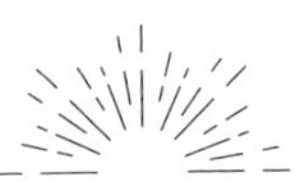

"Remember, no human condition is ever permanent. Then you will not be overjoyed in good fortune nor too scornful in misfortune." SOCRATES

Life is in a constant state of flux. Change is inevitable, and clinging to the illusion of permanence only creates suffering. Today's quote encourages us to embrace impermanence—to find peace in the knowledge that everything is temporary, both the good and the bad.

EMBRACING TRANSCIENCY

Reflect on Change: Think about a time in your life when you experienced a significant change. What was challenging about that experience? What did you learn from it?

Notice the Flow: Take a moment to observe the natural world around you. Notice the changing seasons, the ebb and flow of the tides, the cycle of day and night. Everything is in a state of flux.

Find Freedom in Letting Go: What are you holding on to that is no longer serving you? This might be a past resentment, a limiting belief or a fear of the future. Practice releasing your attachment to these things, knowing that clinging only creates suffering.

I embrace change as a natural part of life. I let go of what no longer serves me and open myself to new possibilities.

DAY 38

"If it is not right, do not do it; if it is not true, do not say it." MARCUS AURELIUS

Integrity is the foundation of a life well-lived, especially in recovery. It's about aligning our actions with our values, even when no one is watching. It's about choosing honesty over convenience, courage over comfort and kindness over cruelty, even when it's difficult.

LIVING WITH INTEGRITY

Define Your Values: What qualities are most important to you; the ones you want to be remembered for?

Check Your Alignment: As you go through your day, pause before making decisions. Ask yourself—

- Is this choice in alignment with my values?
- Will this action bring me closer to or further from the person I want to be?
- Would I be proud to share this choice with someone I respect?

Make Amends When Necessary: If you make a mistake or act out of alignment with your values, acknowledge it. Apologize if appropriate and make amends to the best of your ability.

I choose to live with integrity, aligning my actions with my values and building a life of authenticity and purpose.

DAY 39

"How much better to heal than seek revenge from injury. Vengeance wastes a lot of time and exposes you to many more injuries than the first that sparked it." SENECA

It's easy to get caught in cycles of resentment and anger, especially when we feel we've been wronged. However, seeking revenge or holding on to grudges only keeps us trapped in the past, poisoning our well-being. With the above quote, Seneca reminds us that true strength lies in choosing a different path—the path of forgiveness, compassion and rising above.

CULTIVATING COMPASSION AND FORGIVENESS

Acknowledge Your Feelings: Allow yourself to feel the anger, hurt or resentment you've been carrying. Don't judge yourself for these feelings; simply acknowledge their presence.

Practice Empathy: Try to see the situation from the other person's perspective. This doesn't mean condoning their actions, but seeking to understand the factors that might have contributed to their behavior.

Choose Forgiveness: Forgiveness is a gift you give to yourself. It doesn't mean excusing the other person's actions, rather releasing yourself from the grip of the past.

I choose to forgive others, not because they deserve it, but because I deserve peace. I release the past and embrace the freedom of forgiveness.

DAY 40

"The whole future lies in uncertainty: live immediately."
SENECA

It's easy to get caught up in worries about the future—the fear of relapse, the uncertainty of what lies ahead, the pressure to "get it right." Seneca reminds us that the only moment we truly have is the present one. By embracing the present, we cultivate a sense of peace, gratitude and joy that can sustain us through life's inevitable ups and downs.

PRACTICING MINDFULNESS

Engage Your Senses: Take a moment to bring your full attention to the present experience. What do you see, hear, smell, taste and touch right now?

Focus on Your Breath: Notice the natural rhythm of your breath as you inhale and exhale.

Savor Simple Pleasures: Throughout the day, pause to appreciate the small, often overlooked joys of life—a warm cup of coffee, a beautiful sunset, a moment of laughter.

Be Present in Your Interactions: When you're with others, put away distractions and give them your full attention. Listen with intention and engage authentically.

I am present in this moment. I let go of worries about the future and embrace the peace of the here and now.

DAY 41

"No loss should be more regrettable to us than losing our time, for it's irretrievable." ZENO OF CITIUM

Time is our most precious resource, and the above quote reminds us to value our time with sincerity. In recovery, we must learn to think about time more mindfully, giving respect to each and every second we are blessed with.

MINDFUL SCHEDULING

Examine Your Relationship with Time: Observe how you spend and process time. Do you plan your day in accordance with time? How do you decide the amount of time that is allocated to each activity in your day?

Analyze Your Thinking: Do you find yourself sticking to a plan or the intended allocation? Describe your thinking and reasoning behind this.

Practice Better Habits: Make a list of actions where you spend more or less time than you wish and create a list of steps to make the necessary changes.

I value my time, and I will use my time in a way that makes me happy and healthy.

DAY 42

"If you accomplish something good with hard work, the labor passes quickly but the good endures; if you do something shameful in pursuit of pleasure, the pleasure passes quickly but the shame endures." MUSONIOUS RUFUS

Often, we seek instant gratification and try to achieve this through shortcuts and other ignoble means. But these goals and methods, while tempting in the short term, are unsatisfactory in the long term, and we fall into patterns of seeking what is not good for us. In recovery, we must learn to persevere and wait for the fruits of our labor.

DEVELOPING PATIENCE

Identify Methods and Objectives: Observe wishes and actions that provide short-term fulfillment.

Compare Short-Term to Long-Term Pleasure: Note wishes and actions that provide long-term growth and compare these in value and meaning to their short-term equivalents.

Create a New Path: Find ways to integrate the healthier and happier habits that lead to long-term satisfaction.

I am working toward long-term goals, and these goals will bring more joy than I can imagine.

DAY 43

"When someone is properly grounded in life, they shouldn't have to look outside themselves for approval."
EPICTETUS

Today's quote reminds us that true confidence and self-worth come from within rather than from external sources or societal expectations. When we are grounded in our values and beliefs, we can navigate life with integrity and authenticity.

LOOKING WITHIN

Appreciate Yourself: List qualities you love about yourself and list moments in your life when you were proud of yourself.

Affirm Your Worth: Develop a practice of self-affirmation. Remind yourself of your strengths and accomplishments regularly, reinforcing your self-worth independent of others' opinions.

Engage in Meaningful Activities: Pursue hobbies or projects that align with your values and passions. Engaging in activities that resonate with who you are can help solidify your sense of self.

I am enough. I am built of qualities I value most deeply, and I am working on building those that I am seeking.

DAY 44

"Well-being is realized by small steps, but it is truly no small thing." ZENO OF CITIUM

The above quote emphasizes the significance of incremental progress in achieving a fulfilling life. It encourages us to recognize that meaningful change often comes from consistent, small actions rather than dramatic transformations.

TAKING SMALL STEPS TO ACHIEVE BIG DREAMS

Set Small, Achievable Goals: Break down larger aspirations into manageable tasks. For example, if your goal is to read more, commit to reading just a few pages each day.

Celebrate Small Wins: Acknowledge and celebrate your progress, no matter how minor. This reinforces positive behavior and motivates you to continue.

Stay Committed: Understand that setbacks are a part of the journey. When faced with challenges, remind yourself of the importance of persistence and the cumulative impact of your efforts.

I welcome abundance with an open heart. Every day is full of small wins I deserve.

DAY 45

"You'll never know who you are unless you shed who you pretend to be." VIRONIKA TUGALEVA

Authenticity is essential for personal fulfillment. Pretending to be someone we are not can lead to confusion and dissatisfaction, as it distances us from our true values and desires. In recovery, by shedding these pretenses, we can embrace our individuality and cultivate a life aligned with our authentic selves.

LOSING PRETENSE

Identify Masks: Recognize the roles or personas you adopt in different situations (e.g., at work, with friends). Ask yourself why you feel the need to wear these masks.

Set Boundaries: Learn to say no to situations or people that require you to compromise your true self. Establishing boundaries is crucial in maintaining authenticity.

Meditate on Authenticity: Incorporate mindfulness practices that focus on self-acceptance and authenticity. Guided meditations can help reinforce this mindset.

I embrace my true self with love and acceptance. I release the need for approval from others and confidently express my authentic identity.

DAY 46

"The only true wisdom is in knowing you know nothing."
SOCRATES

It's easy to fall into the trap of thinking we have it all figured out, especially as we progress in our recovery. However, the above quote from Socrates reminds us to approach life with humility and a willingness to learn and grow. We don't have all the answers, and that's okay. It's in acknowledging our limitations that we open ourselves up to new perspectives, greater understanding and deeper wisdom.

CULTIVATING HUMILITY

Acknowledge Your Blind Spots: What are some areas where you might be holding on to rigid beliefs or limiting perspectives?

Seek Out Different Viewpoints: Make an effort to engage with people who have different opinions than your own. Listen with an open mind and a willingness to understand their perspective, even if you don't agree with it.

Embrace Learning: Approach each day as an opportunity to learn something new. Read books, listen to podcasts, engage in conversations that challenge your thinking and never stop seeking growth.

I release the need to be right and embrace the joy of continuous learning. I am a work in progress, and I am open to new perspectives.

DAY 47

"Enjoy present pleasures in such a way as not to injure future ones." SENECA

In the past, our pursuit of pleasure may have been driven by our desire for instant gratification—seeking the quickest and easiest way to feel good, often at the expense of our long-term well-being. Seneca reminds us to approach pleasure with a balanced perspective, considering the potential consequences of our actions and choosing pleasures that nourish us physically, mentally and emotionally.

CHOOSING SUSTAINABLE PLEASURE

Reflect on Your Relationship with Pleasure: What types of activities or experiences bring you joy? Are there any pleasures you tend to overindulge in?

Identify Values-Aligned Pleasures: Make a list of activities that bring you genuine joy and satisfaction that are also aligned with your values and your commitment to sobriety.

Make Conscious Choices: When you're feeling tempted to reach for an unhealthy or unsustainable pleasure, pause and ask yourself—Will this choice bring me joy in the long run? If not, choose a different path.

I choose to engage in activities that bring lasting joy, knowing that true happiness comes from living in alignment with my values.

DAY 48

"You have power over your mind—not outside events. Realize this, and you will find strength."
MARCUS AURELIUS

Life is full of unpredictable events. We may encounter triggers, temptations, setbacks and disappointments. However, we always have the power to choose our response. The above quote from Marcus Aurelius reminds us that true strength lies not in controlling external circumstances but in mastering our own minds.

FINDING INNER STRENGTH

Identify Your Triggers: What situations, people or events tend to trigger negative thoughts, emotions or cravings for you?

Develop a Plan: For each trigger, brainstorm a few healthy coping mechanisms you can use to navigate these challenging moments. This might include—

- Engaging in a physical activity.
- Practicing mindfulness or meditation.
- Removing yourself from the situation.

Visualize Success: Imagine yourself encountering a trigger and successfully navigating it using your chosen coping mechanisms. Visualize yourself feeling strong, centered and in control.

I am not my thoughts or emotions. I am the powerful observer, and I choose to respond to life's challenges with strength and resilience.

DAY 49

"The impediment to action advances action. What stands in the way becomes the way."
MARCUS AURELIUS

We often perceive challenges and obstacles as setbacks on the path to recovery. However, the above quote from Marcus Aurelius encourages us to view obstacles not as roadblocks but as stepping stones. Each challenge we overcome, each craving we resist, each trigger we navigate makes us stronger, more resilient and more deeply committed to our sobriety.

TRANSFORMING OBSTACLES INTO OPPORTUNITIES

Identify the Obstacle: What is a current challenge or obstacle that feels like it's standing in the way of your progress?

Shift Your Perspective: Instead of viewing this obstacle as a defeat, ask yourself—

- What can I learn from this experience?
- How can I use this challenge to strengthen my resolve and build resilience?
- What resources or support systems can I utilize to help me overcome this obstacle?

Create a Plan of Action: Write down three specific, actionable steps you can take today to begin moving through this challenge.

I welcome challenges as opportunities for growth and learning. I am stronger than I think, and I can overcome any obstacle that comes my way.

DAY 50

"If a man knows not to which port he sails, no wind is favorable." SENECA

The above quote is a powerful reminder to live each day with intention and purpose. When we have clarity on our intention or are in the process of seeking clarity, our circumstances will be in favor of us.

LIVING WITH INTENTION

Reflect on Your "Port": What are you hoping to achieve in your life? What qualities do you want to embody? How do you want to be remembered? What kind of life do you wish to live?

Align Your Actions: Take some time to reflect on how well your current actions are aligned with your values and goals. Are there any areas where you may be needing focus? What changes can you make to live more intentionally?

Cherish Each Day: Alongside your goals for your life, find goals and "ports" for each day. Make the most of your time by setting intentions and planning your actions.

I choose to live each day with purpose, making the most of the present moment and creating a life that is meaningful and fulfilling.

DAY 51

"The greatest glory in living lies not in never falling but in rising every time we fall." NELSON MANDELA

The journey of recovery is rarely linear. There will be missteps, setbacks and moments when we stumble. What matters most is our ability to pick ourselves up, learn from our mistakes and continue moving forward with renewed determination.

CULTIVATING RESILIENCE

Reflect on a Setback: Think about a time in your recovery when you faced a challenge or setback. How did you respond in that moment? What helped you move through it?

Identify Your Strengths: What are some of your greatest strengths? List some qualities that have helped you overcome adversity in the past.

Create a Support Plan: Who are the people in your life who offer you unconditional love and support? How can you reach out to them for encouragement when you're facing challenges?

I am resilient, and I am capable of overcoming any challenge that comes my way. I choose to view setbacks as opportunities for growth and learning.

DAY 52

"He is a wise man who does not grieve for the things which he has not but rejoices for those which he has."
EPICTETUS

It's easy to fall into the trap of comparison—focusing on what others have that we don't, whether it's material possessions, career achievements or seemingly effortless sobriety. Epictetus reminds us that true happiness lies in appreciating what we do have—our health, our loved ones, the gift of another day.

CULTIVATING GRATITUDE

Shift Your Focus: Make a conscious effort to notice and appreciate the good in your life, no matter how small. Instead of dwelling on what's lacking, focus on what you have to be grateful for.

Keep a Gratitude Journal: Each day, write down three things you're grateful for. This simple practice can help shift your perspective and cultivate a more positive outlook.

Express Your Appreciation: Don't take the good in your life for granted. Make an effort to express your gratitude to the people you love, for the beauty around you and for the simple gifts of each day.

I am grateful for all the good in my life. I choose to focus on abundance, appreciate the present moment and cultivate a heart full of gratitude.

DAY 53

"When you think you've been injured, apply this rule: If the community isn't injured by it, neither am I. And if it is, anger is not the answer. Show the offender where he went wrong." MARCUS AURELIUS

When we've been hurt or wronged, it's natural to want to seek revenge or act out impulsively. However, Aurelius reminds us that we mustn't lose sight of ourselves and that the consequences of our anger may cause more damage than the cause of our anger. The best course is to rise above, choosing to embody kindness, compassion and integrity.

RESPONDING WITH CARE

Acknowledge Your Feelings: Allow yourself to feel the anger, hurt or resentment you've been carrying. It's important to acknowledge these feelings rather than suppressing them.

Practice Empathy: Try to see the situation from the other person's perspective. This doesn't mean condoning their actions, but seeking to understand the factors that might have contributed to their behavior.

Focus on Your Growth: Instead of dwelling on the past, channel your energy into creating a positive and fulfilling future for yourself. How can you use this experience as a catalyst for personal growth?

I choose to release the weight of the past and embrace the freedom of forgiveness. I choose to move forward with compassion and understanding.

DAY 54

"The journey between what you once were and who you are now becoming is where the dance of life really takes place." BARBARA DE ANGELIS

When we embark on the journey of recovery, it's as if a light has been switched on, illuminating aspects of ourselves and our lives that we may have been avoiding. The above quote reminds us that once we've glimpsed the truth of our own potential and the possibility of a life free from addiction, there's no going back.

HONORING YOUR JOURNEY

Reflect on Your Progress:
Take some time to acknowledge how far you've come on your recovery journey. Celebrate your victories, no matter how small, and honor the strength and resilience you've shown.

Acknowledge Your Challenges:
It's okay to acknowledge the challenges and difficult emotions that arise along the way. Recovery isn't always easy, and it's important to be kind to yourself throughout the process.

Recommit to Your Goals:
What are your reasons for choosing sobriety? What do you hope to achieve in your recovery? Take a moment to reconnect with your motivation and recommit to your goals.

I am proud of myself for choosing sobriety. I am committed to this journey, and I trust in my ability to create a fulfilling and meaningful life.

DAY 55

"There is only one way to happiness and that is to cease worrying about things which are beyond the power of our will." EPICTETUS

We often create unnecessary suffering for ourselves by dwelling on things we cannot control—the past, the actions of others, the future. Epictetus reminds us that true peace comes from focusing our energy on what we can influence—our thoughts, actions and responses.

LETTING GO OF WHAT YOU CANNOT CONTROL

Identify Your Worries: What are you currently worried about, especially in relation to your sobriety?

Distinguish Between What You Can and Cannot Control: For each worry, ask yourself—Is this something I have the power to change? If not, practice releasing your attachment to the outcome.

Shift Your Focus: Once you've identified the things you cannot control, gently redirect your attention to what you can influence—your choices, your actions, your attitude.

I choose to focus on what I can control and release what I cannot. I find freedom in acceptance and peace in the present moment.

DAY 56

"The happiness of those who want to be popular depends on others ... but the happiness of the wise grows out of their own free acts." MARCUS AURELIUS

Often, we seek validation and happiness from external sources—approval from others, material possessions or fleeting highs. Aurelius reminds us that true and lasting happiness comes from within. It's cultivated by aligning our actions with our values, finding contentment in our own company and making choices that nourish our well-being.

CULTIVATING INNER PEACE

Identify External Sources of Validation: Reflect on what you seek validation from outside yourself. Is it recognition, praise or relationships? Acknowledge how these external factors might be influencing your happiness.

Connect with Your Values: What qualities do you want to embody in your life? When your actions align with your values, you cultivate a deep sense of self-respect and inner peace.

Practice Self-Compassion: Treat yourself with the same kindness and understanding that you would offer a close friend. Celebrate your strengths, forgive your mistakes and recognize that you are worthy of happiness just as you are.

My happiness is not dependent on external circumstances. I cultivate inner peace by living in alignment with my values.

DAY 57

"You don't have to control your thoughts. You just have to stop letting them control you." DAN MILLMAN

Our minds are powerful, and sometimes our thoughts can feel like unruly guests, pulling us in different directions. We may experience a whirlwind of anxieties, doubts, cravings or self-criticism. The above quote reminds us that we don't have to believe everything we think. We have the power to observe our thoughts without judgment and choose not to let them dictate our actions.

DETACHING FROM YOUR THOUGHTS

Become an Observer: Imagine your mind is like the sky and your thoughts are clouds passing through. Observe your thoughts without judgment, noticing their patterns and tendencies.

Practice Non-Attachment: You are not your thoughts. Just because a thought arises, doesn't mean you have to believe it, engage with it or let it control you.

Choose Your Focus: You can't always control the thoughts that enter your mind, but you can choose what you focus on. When a negative thought arises, gently redirect your attention to something more positive or productive.

I am not my thoughts. I have the power to observe my thoughts without judgment and to choose which thoughts I engage with.

DAY 58

"The greatest remedy for anger is delay." SENECA

In early recovery, anger can be a powerful emotion which might overwhelm all others. This could be directed toward others who have hurt us, toward ourselves and even toward the challenges of sobriety. Seneca wisely advises us to meet anger with delay, allowing time for the initial intensity to subside before reacting.

CREATING SPACE FOR CALM

Recognize Your Triggers: Become aware of the situations, people or thoughts that tend to evoke anger or irritability in you.

Hit the Pause Button: When you feel anger rising, resist the urge to react immediately. Take a few deep breaths, step away from the situation if possible and give yourself time to cool down.

Choose a Different Path: Once the initial wave of anger has subsided, ask yourself—What is a more skillful way to respond to this situation? Can I communicate my needs or boundaries without resorting to anger? Write out the anger-free methods of communication.

I choose to respond to challenging situations with patience, understanding and compassion. Anger does not control me.

DAY 59

"True wisdom comes to each of us when we realize how little we understand about life, ourselves and the world around us." SOCRATES

It's easy to fall into the trap of thinking we have all the answers, especially as we make progress in our recovery. But Socrates reminds us that true wisdom lies in humility, in acknowledging that we don't know everything and approaching life with an open mind and a willingness to learn.

THINKING LIKE A BEGINNER

Embrace Curiosity: Instead of clinging to fixed beliefs or assumptions, cultivate a sense of curiosity about the world around you.

Ask Questions: Don't be afraid to ask questions, even if you think you "should" know the answer. Seek out knowledge and perspectives that challenge your thinking.

Listen with an Open Mind: When engaging with others, practice active listening. Try to understand their point of view, even if you don't agree with it.

I release the need to be right and embrace the joy of continuous learning. I approach each day with an open mind and a willingness to grow.

DAY 60

"The whole future lies in uncertainty: live immediately."
SENECA

It's easy to get caught up in worries about the future—the fear of relapse, the uncertainty of what lies ahead, the pressure to "get it right." Seneca reminds us that the only moment we truly have is the present one. By embracing the present, we cultivate a sense of peace, gratitude and joy that can sustain us through life's inevitable ups and downs.

SAVORING THE PRESENT MOMENT

Engage Your Senses: Take a few moments to pause and truly connect with your present experience. What do you see, hear, smell, taste and touch right now?

Practice Gratitude: What are you grateful for in this moment? It could be something as simple as a warm cup of coffee, a sunny day or the feeling of your breath moving in and out of your body.

Let Go of Distractions: Put away your phone, step away from screens and create some space for simply being present with yourself and your surroundings.

I am present in this moment. I release worries about the future and embrace the peace of the here and now.

DAY 61

"How much more grievous are the consequences of anger than the causes of it." MARCUS AURELIUS

Anger can lead to actions we later regret, often causing more harm than the original issue. Managing our emotions prevents unnecessary pain. In recovery, developing emotional regulation is key to maintaining healthy relationships and inner peace.

MANAGING ANGER

Recognize Triggers: Identify situations or behaviors that provoke anger.

Pause Before Reacting: When anger arises, take deep breaths and allow yourself some time before you respond.

Reflect and Reframe: Consider the situation from different perspectives to reduce emotional intensity.

I control my responses. By managing anger, I choose peace over conflict.

DAY 62

"If you are distressed by anything external, the pain is not due to the thing itself but to your estimate of it; and this you have the power to revoke at any moment."
MARCUS AURELIUS

It's easy to get caught up in blaming external circumstances for our struggles—stressful situations, challenging relationships or even the availability of substances. Aurelius reminds us that our power lies in how we choose to perceive and respond to these events. We always have the power to reframe our thoughts and choose a more empowering perspective.

REFRAMING CHALLENGING SITUATIONS

Identify the Source of Stress: What is a current situation or event that is causing you stress, anxiety or temptation?

Examine Your Thoughts: What are the thoughts running through your mind about this situation? Are you catastrophizing, assuming the worst or placing blame?

Choose a Different Perspective: Is there another way to view this situation? Could you approach it with more curiosity, compassion or acceptance? How would someone you admire handle this challenge?

I have the power to choose my perspective. I choose thoughts that empower me create a more peaceful experience.

DAY 63

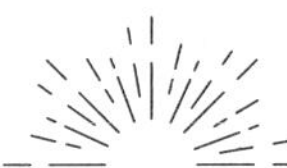

"He who fears death will never do anything worthy of a living man." SENECA

The above quote encourages us to live with courage and intention. It's not about dwelling on death but rather using the awareness of our mortality as a reminder to live each day to the fullest.

LIVING WITH PURPOSE

Reflect on Your Values: What is truly important to you? What kind of person do you want to be? What impact do you want to make on the world?

Set Meaningful Goals: What goals, both big and small, would bring you closer to living in alignment with your values? What steps can you take today to start moving toward these goals?

Make Each Day Count: Approach each day with a sense of purpose and intention. Savor the simple joys, connect with loved ones and engage in activities that bring you meaning and fulfillment.

I choose to live a life of purpose and meaning. I embrace each day as a gift and strive to make a positive impact on the world.

DAY 64

"The impediment to action advances action. What stands in the way becomes the way."
MARCUS AURELIUS

It's natural to view challenges and setbacks as roadblocks on the path to recovery. However, this Stoic principle encourages us to shift our perspective. Often, it's in facing and overcoming obstacles that we discover our greatest strength, resilience and determination.

TRANSFORMING OBSTACLES INTO OPPORTUNITIES

Identify the Obstacle: What is a current challenge or fear that feels like it's holding you back in your recovery?

Reframe Your Perspective: Instead of viewing this obstacle as an insurmountable barrier, try to see it as an opportunity for growth. Ask yourself—

- What can I learn from this experience?
- How can I use this challenge to strengthen my resolve?

Take Action: Break down the challenge into smaller, more manageable steps. What's one small action you can take today to begin moving forward?

I welcome challenges as opportunities for growth. I am stronger than I think, and I am capable of overcoming any obstacle that comes my way.

DAY 65

"You are your own worst enemy. If you can learn to stop expecting impossible perfection, you'll be happier."
EPICTETUS

Our expectations and desire for perfection are often the cause for our anxieties. We create fears based on our presumed shortcomings and the possibility of failure. Today's quote reminds us that we should align our expectations with our needs and abilities, keeping our happiness in focus.

PRACTICING SELF-CARE

Acknowledge Your Humanity: It's okay not to be perfect. Everyone makes mistakes, and setbacks are a natural part of the recovery process.

Treat Yourself with Kindness: Imagine a close friend who is struggling. What would you say to them? Offer yourself the same kindness, compassion and understanding.

Focus on Progress, Not Perfection: Celebrate your accomplishments, no matter how small. Acknowledge how far you've come and the strength you've shown throughout your journey.

I am worthy of love and compassion, especially from myself. I am doing the best I can, and I am proud of myself for choosing recovery.

DAY 66

"The key is to keep company only with people who uplift you, whose presence calls forth your best."
EPICTETUS

The people we surround ourselves with have a profound impact on our thoughts, behaviors and overall well-being. Surrounding ourselves with individuals who support our recovery, inspire us to grow and hold us accountable is crucial for our long-term success.

BUILDING A SUPPORT SYSTEM

Express Appreciation: Take some time today to acknowledge and thank the people in your life who support your recovery journey. Let them know how much their presence means to you.

Set Healthy Boundaries: It's okay to distance yourself from relationships that are no longer serving you, even if it's difficult. Your well-being and sobriety are paramount.

Seek Out New Connections: If you're feeling isolated or unsupported, actively seek out new connections with people who understand your journey. This might involve attending recovery meetings, joining a support group or reaching out to someone you admire.

I am surrounded by love and support. I choose to nurture relationships that uplift me, inspire me and encourage me to be my best self.

DAY 67

"Enjoy present pleasures in such a way as not to injure future ones." SENECA

In the past, our pursuit of pleasure may have been driven by our desire for instant gratification—the quickest and easiest way to feel good, even if it meant sacrificing our long-term well-being. Seneca encourages us to approach pleasure with a balanced perspective—savoring the good things in life, while also considering the potential consequences of our actions.

MAKING CHOICES THAT SUPPORT YOUR FUTURE

Reflect on Your Habits: What are some of your daily habits, routines or choices? Do these choices support your long-term health, happiness and sobriety? Or are there any habits that undermine your well-being?

Set Healthy Boundaries: It's okay to say no to things that don't serve you, even if it means disappointing others. Your recovery is your priority.

Plan for Success: Create a plan for the week ahead that includes activities that nourish your mind, body and spirit. This might include things like exercising, spending time in nature, creative pursuits or connecting with loved ones.

I choose to make choices today that create a brighter and healthier future for myself. I am worthy of a life filled with joy, purpose and fulfillment.

DAY 68

"The obstacle in the path becomes the path. Never forget, within every obstacle is an opportunity to improve our condition." RYAN HOLIDAY

We often view challenges and setbacks as roadblocks on our journey to recovery. However, the above quote from Ryan Holiday encourages us to shift our perspective. Obstacles are not meant to break us; they are opportunities for growth, learning and resilience.

FINDING THE GIFT IN THE CHALLENGE

Identify a Current Challenge: What is a current obstacle or difficulty you're facing in your recovery journey?

Shift Your Perspective: Instead of viewing this challenge as a sign of weakness or failure, try to see it as an opportunity for growth. Ask yourself—

- What can I learn from this experience?
- How can I use this experience to strengthen my resolve?

Focus on What You Can Control: Instead of getting caught up in things you can't control (like the past or the actions of others), focus your energy on what you *can* influence—your attitude, your effort and your choices.

I am stronger than I think. I embrace challenges as opportunities for growth, learning and transformation.

DAY 69

"You have power over your mind—not outside events. Realize this, and you will find strength."
MARCUS AURELIUS

It's easy to feel powerless when facing cravings, triggers or challenging situations. However, Aurelius reminds us that we always have power over our thoughts and our responses. True strength lies in choosing how we react, even when external circumstances feel overwhelming.

RECLAIMING YOUR POWER

Notice Your Triggers: What situations, people, places or emotions tend to trigger cravings, negative thoughts or the urge to engage in unhealthy behaviors?

Develop a Plan: For each trigger, create a plan for how you will respond. This might include—

- Removing yourself from the situation.
- Calling a supportive friend.
- Engaging in a healthy coping mechanism (exercising, meditating, journaling).
- Practicing positive self-talk.

Visualize Success: Imagine yourself encountering this trigger and successfully navigating it using your chosen coping mechanisms. Visualize yourself feeling strong, confident and in control.

I have the power to choose my actions, no matter what challenges life throws my way. I am strong, capable and in control of my choices.

DAY 70

"The happiness of your life depends upon the quality of your thoughts." MARCUS AURELIUS

Our minds are incredibly powerful. The thoughts we habitually entertain shape our emotions, our behaviors and ultimately, our experience of life. Cultivating a positive and compassionate inner dialogue is essential for a happy and fulfilling recovery.

CULTIVATING A POSITIVE MINDSET

Become Aware of Your Self-Talk: Pay attention to the way you talk to yourself throughout the day. Is your inner dialogue kind, encouraging and supportive? Or is it critical, judgmental and self-defeating?

Challenge Negative Thoughts: When you notice negative thoughts or beliefs surfacing, gently challenge their validity. Ask yourself—

- Is this thought really true?
- Is there another, more balanced way to look at this situation?

Choose Empowering Affirmations: Create a list of positive affirmations that resonate with you and support your recovery journey. Repeat these affirmations to yourself throughout the day, especially when you're feeling challenged or discouraged.

I am worthy of love, happiness and recovery. I choose to focus on positive thoughts that empower me and support my well-being.

DAY 71

"How much more harmful are the consequences of anger and grief than the circumstances that aroused them in us." MARCUS AURELIUS

It's easy to get caught in cycles of anger and resentment, especially toward those we feel have wronged us. However, holding on to these feelings only harms us in the long run. Aurelius reminds us that true strength lies in choosing compassion and forgiveness, breaking free from the cycle of negativity.

RELEASING RESENTMENT

Acknowledge Your Feelings: Identify any anger, bitterness or resentment you might be holding toward yourself or others. Allow yourself to feel these emotions without judgment.

Practice Empathy: Try to see the situation from the other person's perspective (even if you don't condone their actions). Everyone makes mistakes; understanding their viewpoint can foster compassion.

Focus on Your Own Growth: Instead of dwelling on the past or seeking retribution, channel your energy toward your own healing and growth. Ask yourself—

- What can I learn from this experience?
- How can I use this to become stronger?

I choose to release the weight of resentment and embrace the freedom of forgiveness. I am committed to my own growth and healing.

DAY 72

"To be like the rock that the waves keep crashing over. It stands unmoved and the raging of the sea falls still around it." MARCUS AURELIUS

The journey of recovery, like life itself, is full of challenges. We will face setbacks, experience difficult emotions and encounter situations that test our resolve. However, these challenges are not meant to break us. They offer opportunities for growth, resilience and self-discovery.

EMBRACING CHALLENGES TO BUILD RESILIENCE

Identify Your Strengths: Think back on a time when you overcame a significant challenge. What strengths did you draw upon? What helped you to persevere?

Reframe Your Perspective: The next time you face a setback in your recovery, try to view it as a chance to learn, grow and become stronger. Ask yourself—What can this experience teach me?

Seek Support: Don't be afraid to ask for help when you need it. Connect with a therapist, sponsor, support group or trusted friend who can offer encouragement and guidance.

I am stronger than I think. I can handle whatever challenges life throws my way. I am committed to my recovery.

DAY 73

"Most powerful is he who has himself in his own power."—SENECA

True power comes from self-mastery. By controlling our impulses and emotions, we navigate life with confidence and clarity. In recovery, cultivating self-discipline empowers us to make choices that align with our goals.

BUILDING SELF-MASTERY

Identify Areas for Improvement: Reflect on aspects of your behavior you'd like to better control.

Set Specific Goals: Create actionable steps to enhance your self-discipline in these areas.

Practice Mindfulness: Increase your awareness of your triggers and habitual reactions to gain greater control over them.

I possess the power of self-mastery. Through discipline, I shape my destiny.

DAY 74

"Waste no more time arguing what a good man should be. Be one." MARCUS AURELIUS

It's easy to get caught up in the "shoulds" of recovery—what we *should* be doing, how we *should* be feeling, who we *should* be. Aurelius cuts through the noise and reminds us that true transformation comes from aligning our actions with our values.

ALIGNING ACTIONS WITH YOUR VALUES

Define Your Values: What qualities are most important to you in your recovery journey? This might include honesty, integrity, compassion, courage or perseverance.

Identify Opportunities for Action: As you go through your day, look for small but meaningful ways to embody these values in your choices and interactions.

Reflect and Adjust: At the end of each day, take a few moments to review your actions. Did you live in accordance with your values? How can you continue to strengthen this alignment tomorrow?

I choose to live with integrity, aligning my actions with my values and creating a life of purpose and meaning.

DAY 75

"People are frugal in guarding their personal property; but as soon as it comes to squandering time, they are most wasteful of the one thing in which it is right to be stingy." SENECA

In life, we tend to be possessive about our belongings and less conscious of how we choose to spend our time, another type of property. Seneca reminds us that time is also something we possess in limited quantities and its value is greater than any material good. In recovery, we must give scrupulous attention to whom we give our time to and how and why we use our time in the way we do.

TREASURING YOUR TIME

Daily Planning: Plan out your day the night before. Pay close attention to how much time each activity requires and how much time you can spare for each.

Observe Distractions: As you start your day, observe where you are able to fully focus and where you tend to get distracted and lose track of time. Find ways to stay conscious about the passing of time, such as setting alarms for specific times of the day.

Mindful Appreciation: Throughout the day, pause to fully take in the simple pleasures and appreciate the joy they bring to your life. Find ways to add more simple pleasures to your life.

II am blessed with an abundance of time that I will cherish and use to the best of my abilities.

DAY 76

"The tranquility that comes when you stop caring what they say. Or think, or do. Only what you do."
MARCUS AURELIUS

It's easy to get caught in the trap of seeking validation from others, especially in early recovery when we're rebuilding our lives and sense of self. Aurelius reminds us that true peace comes from within—from focusing on our own values, actions and growth, rather than being swayed by the opinions or judgments of others.

FINDING SELF-VALIDATION

Identify Your People-Pleasing Tendencies: Do you often find yourself saying yes when you want to say no? Do you worry excessively about what others think of you? Become aware of any patterns of seeking external validation.

Connect with Your Values: What is truly important to *you*? What principles guide your life? When you live in alignment with your values, you cultivate a deep sense of self-respect and inner peace.

Practice Self-Celebration: Acknowledge and celebrate your accomplishments, both big and small. Don't wait for external validation, permit yourself to feel proud of your progress.

My worth is inherent. I am enough, just as I am. I choose to focus on my own growth and celebrate my own victories.

DAY 77

"Progress is impossible without change, and those who cannot change their minds cannot change anything."
GEORGE BERNARD SHAW

Recovery is a journey of transformation, and transformation requires a willingness to change, to let go of old patterns, beliefs and behaviors that no longer serve us. Today's quote reminds us that the key to progress lies in our ability to adapt, evolve and embrace new perspectives.

EMBRACING CHANGE AND GROWTH WITH GRACE

Identify Areas of Resistance: What are you holding on to that might be holding you back in your recovery? This could be a limiting belief, your fear of failure or an unhealthy habit.

Embrace Flexibility: Life is full of unexpected twists and turns. Cultivate a mindset of flexibility and adaptability, knowing that change is a natural part of growth.

Celebrate Small Victories: Progress isn't always linear. Acknowledge and celebrate even the smallest steps forward. Each positive choice you make, no matter how small, is a victory worth celebrating.

I welcome change as an opportunity for growth and expansion. I am constantly evolving, and I trust the journey.

DAY 78

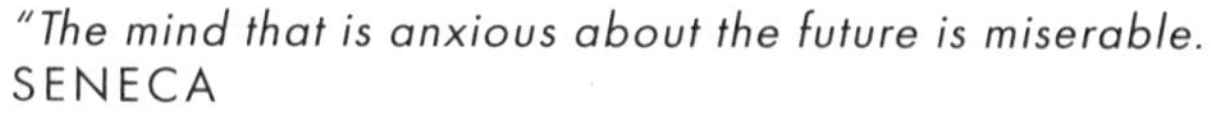

"The mind that is anxious about the future is miserable."
SENECA

It's easy to get caught up in worries about the future—the fear of relapse or the uncertainty of what lies ahead. However, dwelling on these anxieties only creates unnecessary suffering in the present moment. Seneca reminds us to find peace by focusing on what we can control—our actions, our choices and our attitude *today*.

GROUNDING YOURSELF IN THE PRESENT

Engage Your Senses: When you notice your mind racing with worries about the future, take a few moments to ground yourself in the present moment. Notice the sights, sounds, smells, tastes and sensations around you.

Focus on Your Breath: Your breath is a powerful anchor to the present. Notice the natural rhythm of your breath as you inhale and exhale.

Practice Gratitude: Shift your focus from worry to appreciation. What are you grateful for in this moment? This simple practice can help calm your mind and cultivate a sense of peace.

I choose to focus on the present moment, releasing worries about the future and finding peace in the here and now.

DAY 79

"It is not the man who has too little but the man who craves more that is poor." SENECA

In our consumerist culture, it's easy to fall into the trap of thinking that happiness lies in acquiring more—more possessions, more achievements, more experiences. However, Seneca reminds us that true contentment comes from appreciating what we have and finding joy in simplicity.

CHASING CONTENTMENT

Practice Gratitude: Take some time to appreciate all the good in your life—your health, your loved ones, your home, the beauty of nature. Write a gratitude list, send "thank you" notes or simply reflect on your blessings.

Simplify Your Life: Are there areas of your life where you feel overwhelmed or bogged down by possessions or commitments? Consider simplifying. Let go of what you don't truly need or enjoy.

Find Joy in the Simple Things: Make a conscious effort to savor the small pleasures of life—a walk in nature, a good book, a conversation with a friend, a delicious meal.

I have everything I need to be happy right now. I choose to focus on abundance and cultivate a heart full of gratitude.

DAY 80

"The only true wisdom is in knowing you know nothing."
SOCRATES

It's easy to approach recovery with a sense of urgency, feeling like we need to have all the answers, fix all our problems and achieve perfect sobriety overnight. Socrates's words remind us to approach this journey with humility, recognizing that we don't have all the answers and embracing the transformative power of a beginner's mind.

APPROACHING RECOVERY WITH CURIOSITY

Release the Need to Be Right: Let go of the need to have all the answers or to appear "perfect" in your recovery. Embrace the unknown with a sense of curiosity and openness.

Ask Questions: Don't be afraid to ask for help, guidance or support when you need it. Reach out to a therapist, sponsor, support group or a trusted friend.

Embrace Mistakes as Learning Opportunities: Recovery is a journey, not a destination. There will be missteps along the way. Instead of judging yourself harshly, view these experiences as opportunities for learning and growth.

I am a work in progress, and that's okay. I embrace the journey of recovery with an open mind and a willingness to learn and grow.

DAY 81

"It's not what happens to you, but how you react to it that matters." EPICTETUS

Our minds are powerful. The thoughts we habitually focus on shape our emotions, behaviors and overall well-being. By learning to consciously choose our thoughts, especially in challenging situations, we can manage stress, reduce cravings and cultivate a more positive and resilient mindset.

SHIFTING YOUR FOCUS

Become Aware of Your Thoughts: Pay close attention to your inner dialogue throughout the day. What types of thoughts tend to dominate your mind—positive, negative or neutral? Simply observe without judgment.

Interrupt Negative Thought Patterns: When you notice negative, self-critical or fear-based thoughts, gently acknowledge them and then consciously choose to shift your focus.

Focus on What You Can Control: Direct your attention to what you *can* influence—your actions, your attitude and your choices in the present moment.

I have the power to choose my thoughts. I choose thoughts that empower me and create a more peaceful inner world.

DAY 82

"The greatest blessings of mankind are within us and within our reach. A wise man is content with his lot, whatever it may be, without wishing for what he has not." SENECA

With today's quote, Seneca wisely reminds us that true contentment lies in embracing the present moment. Dwelling on the past or worrying about the future steals our joy and keeps us trapped in a cycle of negativity. Finding peace and happiness in the here and now is key to living a fulfilling life in recovery.

SAVORING THE PRESENT MOMENT

Engage Your Senses: Throughout the day, pause to notice the simple pleasures around you—the warmth of the sun on your skin, the taste of your morning coffee, the sound of a loved one's laughter.

Practice Mindfulness Meditation: Even a few minutes of mindful breathing can help calm your mind, ground you in the present and cultivate a sense of inner peace.

Let Go of What You Cannot Control: Focus your energy on what you can influence—your actions, your choices, your attitude—and release your grip on things you cannot change.

I choose to embrace the present moment, finding joy in the simple things and releasing worries about the past or future.

DAY 83

"So other people hurt me? That's their problem. Their character and actions are not mine. What is done to me is ordained by nature, what I do by my own."
MARCUS AURELIUS

When we've been hurt or wronged, it's natural to feel anger, resentment or even a desire for revenge. However, these feelings keep us trapped in a cycle of negativity and pain. Aurelius reminds us that true strength lies in acknowledging that others act based on their own internal problems in their internal world and that we have our own world to care for.

FOCUSING ON YOURSELF

Acknowledge Your Feelings: Allow yourself to feel the anger, hurt or resentment you're experiencing. It's important to acknowledge these emotions rather than suppressing them.

Practice Empathy: Try to see the situation from the other person's perspective. This can help cultivate compassion and understanding.

Focus on Your Growth: Channel your energy into creating a positive and fulfilling future for yourself. Ask yourself—How can I use this experience as a catalyst for personal growth? Implement the answer in your everyday life.

I choose to let go of anger and resentment. I embrace forgiveness and compassion, for myself and for others.

DAY 84

"Life is neither good nor bad but only a place for good and bad." MARCUS AURELIUS

In life, fulfilling and distressing moments will always occur, and while these are only temporary moments, it is in our power how we reflect on these moments and how they affect our lives. In recovery, we must work toward accepting all that comes our way, good and bad, while also choosing which moments we take lessons from and which ones we let pass without allowing them to derail us.

ACCEPTING THE DUALITY OF EVERYDAY LIFE

Become Aware of Your Thoughts: Throughout the day, simply notice the thoughts that arise in your mind. When things happen, how often do you assign the labels "good" and "bad" to events?

Examine Your Labeling: How do these labels affect how you judge your day? Do you hold onto the negative feelings caused by an event labeled "bad"?

Creating Balance: In your life, do you tend to use the "bad" label more than "good"? If yes, reflect on what events you assign the "good" label to. How can you work toward creating a balance?

Life is beautiful, and I accept the good and the bad with an open mind, knowing that I can stand my ground through anything.

DAY 85

"Meditate often on the interconnectedness and mutual interdependence of all things in the universe."
MARCUS AURELIUS

We are all intrinsically connected to each other, and our actions affect everyone around us. Surrounding ourselves with individuals who support our growth, inspire us to be our best selves and hold us accountable is crucial for a fulfilling life in recovery.

NURTURING A SUPPORTIVE COMMUNITY

Take Inventory of Your Relationships: Reflect on the people you spend the most time with. Do they support your recovery, inspire you to grow and encourage you to be your best self? Or do they drain your energy, trigger unhealthy behaviors or hold you back?

Observe Yourself: Reflect on yourself in relation to the same people. Do you support their recovery, inspire them to grow and encourage them to be their best self?

Set Intentions and Healthy Boundaries: Review your reflections. Who are the people you should spend more time with and what are steps you can take to develop a relationship that is mutually uplifting? Similarly, are there people that you would benefit to reduce time with and work toward self-preservation?

I am part of a thriving, healthy community, and I choose to bring goodness to the lives of others.

DAY 86

"He who is brave is free." SENECA

Choosing sobriety is an act of courage. It takes bravery to confront our fears, to break free from unhealthy patterns and to build a new life. Every day we choose courage over comfort, we step closer to freedom—freedom from addiction, freedom from self-sabotage and freedom to live a life aligned with our values.

STEPPING OUTSIDE YOUR COMFORT ZONE

Identify an Area of Growth: What is one area of your life where you'd like to grow, change or step outside your comfort zone? This could be related to your recovery, your relationships, your career or any aspect of your personal development.

Choose a Small Act of Courage: What's one small step you can take today to move toward this goal? It doesn't have to be a huge leap, even a small act of courage can build momentum and confidence.

Celebrate Your Bravery: Acknowledge and celebrate your willingness to step outside your comfort zone. Each act of courage, no matter how small, strengthens your resilience.

I am brave. I choose courage over comfort. I am capable of creating the life I desire.

DAY 87

"There is only one way to happiness and that is to cease worrying about things which are beyond the power of our will." EPICTETUS

We often create unnecessary suffering for ourselves by focusing on things we cannot control—the past, the actions of others or the unpredictable nature of life. Epictetus reminds us that true peace and happiness come from surrendering to what *is*, releasing what we cannot change and focusing our energy on what we can influence—our own thoughts, actions and responses.

PRACTICING ACCEPTANCE

Identify Areas of Resistance: What are you currently resisting in your life? What situation, emotion or thought are you fighting against?

Choose to Surrender: Instead of engaging in a futile battle with reality, practice acceptance. Acknowledge the truth of the situation, even if you don't like it. This doesn't mean you have to concede defeat, it simply means that you choose to stop resisting what is.

Shift Your Focus: Once you've practiced acceptance, gently redirect your attention to what you can control—your attitude, your effort and your choices in the present moment.

I choose to accept what is, release what I cannot control and find peace in the present moment.

DAY 88

"The greatest wealth is to live content with little." PLATO

In our consumer-driven society, it's easy to get caught in the trap of believing that happiness lies in acquiring more—more possessions, more achievements, more experiences. However, Plato reminds us that true wealth and contentment come from appreciating the abundance we already have and finding joy in simplicity.

PURSUING CONTENTMENT

Shift Your Focus: Make a conscious effort to notice and appreciate the good things in your life, no matter how small. Focus on what you have, not on what you lack.

Simplify Your Surroundings: Are there areas of your life where you feel overwhelmed or bogged down by possessions or commitments? Consider simplifying. Let go of what you don't truly need or enjoy.

Find Joy in the Ordinary: Practice finding moments of joy and beauty in the everyday—a walk in nature, a good book, a conversation with a loved one.

I have everything I need to be happy right now. I choose to focus on abundance and cultivate a heart full of gratitude.

DAY 89

"Reason gives time to either side, and then demands a further adjournment to give itself room to tease out the truth: anger is in a hurry." SENECA

Anger is a natural emotion but when left unchecked, it can become destructive—both to ourselves and to those around us. In recovery, managing anger is crucial because it can trigger cravings or lead to relapse. With today's quote, Seneca reminds us that by simply delaying our response, we give ourselves the opportunity to choose a more measured and constructive reaction.

ART OF DELAYED RESPONSE

Recognize Immediate Reactions: Pay attention to the physical and emotional signs of rising anger—tightness in your chest, clenched fists, a sudden rush of heat.

Implement a Cooling-Off Period: Commit to a personal rule of waiting before responding when angry. This could be counting to thirty, taking five deep breaths or stepping outside for fresh air.

Reflect Before Responding: Use this pause to consider the bigger picture. Ask yourself—Is this worth my peace? How can I respond in a way that aligns with my values and supports my recovery? Apply the answers to the situation.

I choose patience over impulse. By embracing calm, I maintain control over my actions and nurture my well-being.

DAY 90

"Everything can be taken from a man but one thing: the last of the human freedoms—to choose one's attitude in any given set of circumstances." VIKTOR FRANKL

Our attitudes and beliefs have the power to shape our reality. If we doubt our ability to maintain sobriety, to overcome challenges or to create a fulfilling life, those doubts can become self-fulfilling prophecies. Conversely, if we cultivate beliefs that empower us, support our growth and inspire us to reach for our potential, we pave the way for a brighter future.

CULTIVATING BELIEFS THAT EMPOWER YOU

Identify Limiting Beliefs: What are some of the negative or limiting beliefs you hold about yourself, your recovery or your future?

Challenge Those Beliefs: Gently question the validity of these beliefs. Are they based on facts or on old patterns of thinking? What evidence is there to support or refute these beliefs?

Choose Empowering Beliefs: Once you've identified and challenged your limiting beliefs, consciously choose to replace them with more empowering ones. Write down affirmations that reflect these new beliefs and repeat them to yourself daily.

I am capable of achieving anything I set my mind to. I believe in my ability to create a joyful, fulfilling and sober life for myself.

DAY 91

"The greatest discovery of all time is that a person can change his future by merely changing his attitude."
OPRAH WINFREY

Our attitude shapes our experience of life, especially in recovery. Approaching challenges with a positive, optimistic outlook can make all the difference in maintaining sobriety and navigating difficult emotions.

SHIFTING YOUR OUTLOOK

Notice Your Default Setting: What is your typical attitude when faced with challenges or setbacks? Do you tend to focus on the negative, anticipate the worst or blame yourself or others?

Choose a More Empowering Perspective: Consciously shift your focus to a more positive, hopeful or solution-oriented perspective. Ask yourself—

- What's one good thing about this situation?
- What can I learn from this experience?
- What's within my control to change?

Practice Gratitude: Even amid difficulties, there's always something to be grateful for. Take a few moments to appreciate the good in your life—your health, your loved ones, your recovery.

I choose to approach life with optimism and gratitude. I believe in my ability to overcome challenges and create a brighter future.

DAY 92

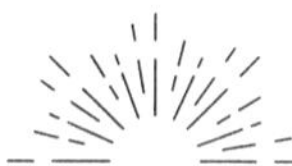

"The soul becomes dyed with the color of its thoughts."
MARCUS AURELIUS

Our thoughts have a profound impact on who we are and who we are becoming. Just as a dye can permanently color a fabric, the thoughts we habitually entertain shape our beliefs, our emotions and our actions. Cultivating a positive and compassionate inner dialogue is essential for a vibrant and fulfilling life in recovery.

CULTIVATING POSITIVE SELF-TALK

Become Aware of Your Inner Critic: Pay attention to the way you talk to yourself, especially when facing challenges or setbacks. Is your inner voice critical, judgmental and harsh? Or is it kind, encouraging and compassionate?

Challenge Negative Thoughts: When you notice negative self-talk, challenge those thoughts. Are they based on facts or on old, limiting beliefs? What's a more balanced way to view this situation?

Replace with Positive Affirmations: Create a list of affirmations that resonate with you and reflect your desired state of being. Repeat these affirmations to yourself regularly, especially when you notice negative thoughts creeping in.

I choose to speak to myself with kindness and encouragement. I am worthy of love, respect and support, especially from myself.

DAY 93

"The only person you are destined to become is the person you decide to be." RALPH WALDO EMERSON

We are not defined by our past mistakes or by the challenges we face in recovery. We have the power to choose who we want to be and to create the life we desire.

FINDING YOUR IDEAL SELF

Connect with Your Vision: Take some time to imagine yourself living a fulfilling and meaningful life in recovery. What are you doing? Who are you with? How do you feel? Engage all your senses as you create a vivid picture in your mind.

Identify the Qualities: What qualities do you embody in this vision? Are you confident, compassionate, resilient, creative? Write down the characteristics that resonate most strongly with you.

Take Aligned Action: What steps can you take today to move closer to this vision? What choices, habits or actions would be in alignment with your ideal self?

I am the architect of my own life. I choose to create a future filled with purpose, joy and fulfillment.

DAY 94

"It's not what happens to you but how you react to it that matters." EPICTETUS

Life is full of unexpected twists and turns. We will inevitably encounter challenges, setbacks and disappointments. However, we always have the power to choose our response. This choice—how we react to adversity—is what ultimately shapes our experience.

REPLYING WITH RESILIENCE

Identify Your Triggers: What situations, people or emotions tend to trigger negative or unhelpful reactions in you? Become aware of your patterns and be prepared for these moments.

Practice the Pause: When you encounter a trigger, hit the pause button before reacting. Take a few deep breaths, create some distance from the situation if possible and give yourself time to choose a more skillful response.

Choose a Different Path: Ask yourself—What is a more helpful way to respond to this situation? How can I communicate my needs or boundaries calmly and assertively? Write the answers down and apply them in appropriate situations.

I am not my reactions. I have the power to choose my response, and I choose responses that support my well-being and align with my values.

DAY 95

"Very little is needed to make a happy life; it is all within yourself, in your way of thinking."
MARCUS AURELIUS

True and lasting happiness doesn't come from external circumstances, material possessions or the approval of others. It comes from within—from cultivating a peaceful mind, a grateful heart and a life aligned with our values.

CULTIVATING INNER PEACE

Practice Gratitude: Take some time to reflect on all the good in your life—your health, your loved ones, your recovery, the simple pleasures that bring you joy. Write a gratitude list, express your appreciation to someone you love or simply savor a moment of beauty.

Simplify Your Life: Are there areas of your life where you feel overwhelmed or bogged down by possessions, commitments or obligations? Consider simplifying. Let go of what you don't truly need or enjoy.

Connect with Nature: Spending time in nature has a profound ability to calm the mind, nourish the soul and bring us back to a place of peace.

I carry peace within me. I choose to focus on gratitude, simplify my life and connect with the beauty around me.

DAY 96

"The man who moves a mountain begins by carrying away small stones." CONFUCIUS

Overcoming addiction and creating a fulfilling life in recovery can feel like a monumental task. The above quote reminds us that even the greatest achievements are accomplished one step at a time. Focus on making small, consistent efforts each day, and you'll gradually build the momentum you need to reach your goals.

TAKING SMALL STEPS

Break Down Your Goals: What is one big goal you're working toward in your recovery? Break it down into smaller, more manageable steps.

Focus on Today: Instead of getting overwhelmed by the enormity of your goals, focus on what you can do *today*. What's one small action you can take to move yourself closer to your goal?

Celebrate Your Progress: Acknowledge and celebrate each step you take, no matter how small. Each act of effort is a victory worth recognizing.

I am capable of achieving great things. I choose to focus on consistent effort, celebrate small victories and trust in the process of growth.

DAY 97

"The only thing that stands between you and your dream is the will to try and the belief that it is actually possible." JOEL BROWN

Our beliefs have the power to shape our reality. If we doubt our ability to create a fulfilling and sober life, those doubts can become self-fulfilling prophecies. However, if we cultivate beliefs that empower us, support our growth and inspire us to reach for our potential, we open ourselves to a world of possibilities.

CULTIVATING BELIEFS THAT EMPOWER YOU

Identify Limiting Beliefs: What are some of the negative or limiting beliefs you hold about yourself, your recovery or your future?

Challenge the Validity: Gently question these beliefs. Are they based on facts or on old patterns of thinking that may no longer serve you? What evidence is there to support or refute these beliefs?

Choose Empowering Beliefs: Once you've identified and challenged your limiting beliefs, consciously choose to replace them with more empowering ones. Write down affirmations that reflect these new beliefs and repeat them to yourself regularly.

I am capable of achieving my dreams. I believe in myself, my strength and my ability to create a fulfilling life.

DAY 98

"If you really want to escape the things that harass you, what you're needing is not to be in a different place but to be a different person." SENECA

It's easy to think that changing our external circumstances—our job, our relationships, our location—will bring us lasting happiness and peace. However, Seneca reminds us that true transformation comes from within. It's not about changing our environment but about changing ourselves.

FOCUSING ON INNER TRANSFORMATION

Identify Your Patterns: What are some of your habitual thoughts, behaviors or reactions that might be contributing to your struggles?

Choose Different Responses: Instead of reacting on autopilot, practice pausing, observing your impulses and making a conscious choice about how you want to respond.

Cultivate Self-Awareness: Pay attention to your thoughts, emotions and behaviors throughout the day. The more aware you are of your patterns, the more empowered you become to choose differently.

I choose to focus on my own growth and transformation. I am committed to becoming the best version of myself.

DAY 99

"The best and most beautiful things in the world cannot be seen or even touched—they must be felt with the heart."
HELEN KELLER

In our pursuit of a fulfilling life in recovery, it's easy to get caught up in external achievements and material possessions. Helen Keller's words remind us to cultivate the qualities that truly matter—love, compassion, gratitude, connection and inner peace.

CONNECTING WITH YOUR HEART

Practice Gratitude: Take some time to reflect on the people, experiences and blessings in your life that fill your heart with gratitude.

Cultivate Compassion: Offer kindness and understanding, both to yourself and to others. Practice forgiveness, empathy and kindness.

Connect with Nature: Spend time in nature, allowing its beauty and serenity to nourish your soul.

Engage in Activities You Love: Make time for activities that bring you joy, spark your creativity and nurture your spirit.

I am a being of love and light. I choose to live from my heart, connect with others authentically and cultivate inner peace.

DAY 100

"He who is brave is free." SENECA

Courage isn't the absence of fear; it's the decision to act despite it. In recovery, bravery is required to face our vulnerabilities, to confront past mistakes and to step into a new way of living. By embracing courage, we liberate ourselves from the chains of fear and open the door to true freedom.

EMBRACING COURAGE IN RECOVERY

Identify Your Fears: Write down the fears that are holding you back—whether it's fear of failure, rejection or the unknown.

Take Small Brave Steps: Choose one fear to confront today. It doesn't have to be monumental; even small acts of courage build momentum. For example, have an honest conversation, attend a social event sober or try a new activity.

Reflect on the Outcome: At the end of the day, journal about how facing this fear made you feel. Did it empower you? What did you learn about yourself?

I am courageous and capable. Each brave step I take leads me closer to the freedom I seek.

DAY 101

"Waste no more time arguing what a good person should be. Be one." MARCUS AURELIUS

It's easy to get caught up in overthinking or debating what it means to be good or to live well. With the above quote, Marcus Aurelius urges us to stop theorizing and start embodying our ideals. In recovery, this means living our values through our actions, making choices that reflect who we aspire to be.

LIVING YOUR VALUES

Define Your Core Values: List the top five values that are most important to you—honesty, compassion, integrity, etc.

Align Actions with Values: Reflect on your daily activities and decisions. Are they in harmony with your core values? Identify any discrepancies.

Set Intentional Actions: Choose one action today that directly expresses one of your core values. Make a conscious effort to implement it.

I live my values boldly and authentically. My actions speak the truth of who I am.

DAY 102

"Man is not worried by real problems so much as by his imagined anxieties about real problems." EPICTETUS

Our minds have a tendency to catastrophize, creating worst-case scenarios that may never happen. This mental habit can cause unnecessary anxiety and stress, which can be detrimental in recovery. Recognizing this, we can learn to distinguish between imagined fears and actual challenges, freeing ourselves from undue suffering.

GROUNDING YOURSELF IN REALITY

Identify Worrisome Thoughts: Notice when you're feeling anxious or stressed. What imagined scenarios are contributing to these feelings?

Challenge Your Imagination: Ask yourself—What evidence do I have that this will happen? Is there a more likely or positive outcome?

Focus on the Present Moment: Engage in mindfulness practices such as deep breathing, meditation or grounding exercises to bring your attention back to the here and now.

I release unfounded fears and embrace the present. I trust in my ability to handle whatever comes my way.

DAY 103

"The happiness of your life depends upon the quality of your thoughts." MARCUS AURELIUS

Our thoughts shape our perceptions, influence our emotions and ultimately determine our experiences. In recovery, cultivating positive and constructive thinking patterns can significantly enhance our well-being and resilience. By nurturing a mindset focused on growth and gratitude, we pave the way for a fulfilling life.

CULTIVATING POSITIVE THOUGHT PATTERNS

Monitor Your Thoughts: Throughout the day, observe your internal dialogue. Are your thoughts generally positive, neutral or negative?

Reframe Negative Thoughts: When you catch yourself thinking negatively, pause and consciously reframe the thought into a more positive or realistic perspective.

Practice Daily Gratitude: At the end of the day, write down three things you're grateful for. This practice trains your mind to focus on the good in your life.

I choose thoughts that empower and uplift me. My mind is a source of peace and joy.

DAY 104

"Wealth consists not in having great possessions but in having few wants." EPICTETUS

In a world driven by consumerism and the pursuit of more, it's easy to fall into the trap of thinking that accumulating possessions or achievements will bring us happiness. Epictetus reminds us that true wealth is not about external abundance but about inner contentment. In recovery, learning to be satisfied with what we have can lead to greater peace and fulfillment.

CHASING CONTENTMENT

Assess Your Desires: Reflect on areas in your life where you feel a constant need for more—be it material items, recognition or even personal achievements. Write them down.

Focus on Gratitude: For each desire you've listed, identify something you already have that fulfills a similar need. Practice gratitude for these existing blessings.

Simplify Your Life: Choose one area where you can reduce excess or simplify. This might mean decluttering your space, limiting time on social media or setting boundaries to protect your time and energy.

I find richness in simplicity and abundance in gratitude. My true wealth lies within.

DAY 105

"Life is long if you know how to use it." SENECA

Clarity of purpose is essential for meaningful progress. Epictetus encourages us to define our aspirations before taking action. In recovery, envisioning the person you want to become can guide your daily choices and reinforce your commitment to change.

DEFINING YOUR PATH

Envision Your Future Self: Spend time visualizing who you want to be in your recovery journey. Consider your values, behaviors and the impact you wish to have on others.

Set Clear Goals: Based on your vision, outline specific, achievable goals that will move you toward becoming that person. Break them down into short-term and long-term objectives.

Create an Action Plan: Identify concrete steps you can take today and in the coming weeks to advance toward your goals. Commit to taking at least one of these steps today.

I am the creator of my destiny. By aligning my actions with my vision, I become who I aspire to be.

DAY 106

"Some of the wisest of men have in consequence of this called anger a short madness: for it is equally devoid of self-control, regardless of decorum." SENECA

When we are wronged, the instinct to retaliate can be strong. However, mirroring negative behaviors only perpetuates harm. Seneca advises that the most powerful response is to uphold our own principles and refuse to be pulled into negativity. In recovery, this mindset protects our peace and integrity.

RISING ABOVE NEGATIVITY AND IMPULSES

Identify Negative Influences: Think about individuals or situations that provoke negative reactions in you. Acknowledge how they affect your emotions and behaviors.

Define Your Values: Reaffirm the values that are important to you—kindness, honesty, respect—and consider how you can embody them even in challenging interactions.

Practice Compassionate Detachment: When confronted with negativity, choose to respond (or refrain from responding) in a way that reflects your values. This might mean setting boundaries, walking away or responding with kindness.

I choose to act with integrity, regardless of others' actions. My character is defined by my choices.

DAY 107

"You have power over your mind—not outside events. Realize this, and you will find strength."
MARCUS AURELIUS

External circumstances are often beyond our control, but our thoughts and attitudes are within our domain. By focusing on managing our internal responses, we empower ourselves to navigate life's unpredictability with grace. In recovery, this internal locus of control is a cornerstone of resilience.

STRENGTHENING YOUR MENTAL FORTITUDE

Acknowledge Uncontrollable External Events: List situations causing you stress or concern that are outside your control.

Focus on Your Response: For each situation, identify how you can manage your thoughts or behaviors in response. What mindset will help you cope effectively?

Develop a Mindfulness Routine: Incorporate practices like meditation, deep breathing or journaling to enhance your awareness of your own thoughts and cultivate a calm mind.

I harness the power of my mind to create my experience. Inner strength is my steadfast ally.

DAY 108

"He who laughs at himself never runs out of things to laugh at." EPICTETUS

Embracing humor and the ability to laugh at ourselves can diffuse tension and foster joy. It reminds us not to take ourselves too seriously and to find lightness even in imperfections. In recovery, this attitude can alleviate stress and promote a positive outlook.

EMBRACING HUMOR AND SELF-ACCEPTANCE

Reflect on a Humbling Experience: Think of a recent moment where things didn't go as planned. Find the humor in the situation and note what you learned.

Share a Lighthearted Moment: Connect with someone you trust and share a funny story or joke. Laughter strengthens bonds and elevates mood.

Practice Self-Compassion: When you make mistakes, remind yourself that imperfection is part of being human. Replace self-criticism with gentle humor.

I embrace life with a light heart. Joy and laughter are integral parts of my journey.

DAY 109

"It does not matter what you bear but how you bear it."
SENECA

Challenges are an inevitable part of life, but our approach to them defines our experience. Seneca highlights that facing hardships with dignity and resilience is more significant than the hardship itself. In recovery, adopting a courageous and steadfast attitude can transform obstacles into stepping stones.

CULTIVATING RESILIENCE

Recall Past Resilience: Reflect on a time when you faced adversity and persevered. What qualities did you exhibit?

Adopt Empowering Beliefs: Affirm your ability to handle difficulties. Replace thoughts of doubt with statements of strength and capability.

Support Others: Offering encouragement to someone else facing challenges can reinforce your own resilience and foster a sense of connection.

I face life's trials with courage and grace. My spirit remains unshaken by adversity.

DAY 110

"Be tolerant with others and strict with yourself."
MARCUS AURELIUS

Today's quote encourages us to extend understanding and patience to others while holding ourselves accountable to high standards. It fosters personal growth and harmonious relationships. In recovery, this mindset helps us build empathy and maintain integrity without projecting our expectations on to others.

BALANCING COMPASSION AND ACCOUNTABILITY

Evaluate Expectations: Notice if you hold others to standards they may not be aware of or capable of meeting. Reflect on how this affects your relationships.

Set Personal Goals: Identify areas where you can improve or be more disciplined in your behavior. Create an action plan to address these areas.

Practice Empathy: When interacting with others, strive to understand their perspectives and circumstances. Offer support rather than judgment.

I strive for excellence within myself and extend compassion to others. Through this balance, I contribute to a more understanding world.

DAY 111

"No man is free who is not master of himself."
EPICTETUS

True freedom comes from self-mastery—the ability to govern our thoughts, emotions and actions. In recovery, gaining control over ourselves empowers us to break free from the chains of addiction. By cultivating discipline and self-awareness, we reclaim our autonomy and chart a course toward a fulfilling life.

MASTERING SELF-CONTROL

Set Personal Boundaries: Identify areas where you struggle with self-control. Establish clear boundaries to help manage temptations or triggers.

Practice Mindful Decision-Making: Before acting, pause to consider whether your choice aligns with your long-term goals and values.

Build Healthy Habits: Introduce routines that promote well-being, such as regular exercise, balanced nutrition or consistent sleep patterns.

I am the master of my thoughts and actions. Through self-control, I attain true freedom.

DAY 112

"Difficulty shows what men are." EPICTETUS

Challenges reveal our true character. It's in moments of adversity that we discover our strengths and weaknesses. In recovery, facing difficulties head-on allows us to grow and build resilience. Each obstacle becomes an opportunity to demonstrate courage and reinforce our commitment to change.

EMBRACING CHALLENGES

Reflect on Recent Challenges: Identify a difficulty you've faced recently. Consider how you responded and what it revealed about you.

Learn from Adversity: Determine what lessons you can take away from the experience. How can it inform your future actions?

Adopt a Growth Mindset: Embrace challenges as opportunities for development rather than setbacks. Affirm your ability to overcome obstacles.

Challenges strengthen me. I face them with courage and emerge wiser.

DAY 113

"Be as you wish to seem." SOCRATES

Authenticity involves aligning our outward behavior with our inner values and aspirations. Pretending to be someone we're not leads to internal conflict and hinders genuine connections. In recovery, embracing our true selves fosters self-acceptance and builds trust with others.

LIVING AUTHENTICALLY

Identify Discrepancies: Reflect on areas where your actions may not align with your true self or values.

Embrace Vulnerability: Allow yourself to be seen as you are, acknowledging both strengths and areas for growth.

Align Actions with Intentions: Make conscious choices that reflect your authentic self, even if they require stepping outside your comfort zone.

I honor my true self. By being authentic, I live with integrity and purpose.

DAY 114

"The only constant in life is change." HERACLITUS

Change is an inevitable part of existence. Resisting it can lead to suffering, while embracing it opens the door to growth and new possibilities. In recovery, accepting change allows us to adapt, heal and evolve beyond our past selves.

EMBRACING TRANSIENCY

Acknowledge Life's Transience:
Reflect on how things have changed over time in your life—relationships, circumstances, personal beliefs.

Let Go of Attachments:
Identify any areas where you're clinging to the past or resisting change. Practice releasing these attachments.

Welcome New Beginnings:
Approach change with curiosity and openness, viewing it as an opportunity for renewal.

I embrace change as a natural part of life. Through adaptability, I find strength and growth.

DAY 115

"Well-being is attained by little and little, and nevertheless is no little thing itself." ZENO OF CITIUM

Progress is often gradual. Small, consistent efforts accumulate over time to create significant transformation. In recovery, patience and persistence are key. Recognizing and celebrating incremental achievements keeps us motivated on our journey toward well-being.

CELEBRATING SMALL VICTORIES

Track Your Progress: Write down recent accomplishments, no matter how minor they may seem.

Set Micro-Goals: Establish achievable daily or weekly objectives that contribute to your larger recovery goals.

Reward Yourself: Find healthy ways to acknowledge your efforts—treat yourself to a favorite activity or share your success with a supportive friend.

Each small step I take leads to meaningful progress. I honor my journey and growth.

DAY 116

"Man conquers the world by conquering himself."
ZENO OF CITIUM

True conquest is not about exerting control over external circumstances but mastering our inner world. By overcoming our fears, doubts and destructive habits, we empower ourselves to navigate life with confidence and purpose. In recovery, self-mastery is the path to lasting fulfillment.

SELF-MASTERY

Identify Internal Obstacles: Recognize personal challenges such as negative self-talk, procrastination or unhealthy coping mechanisms.

Develop Self-Discipline: Choose one area to focus on improving. Create a plan to address it with practical steps.

Practice Mindfulness: Cultivate an awareness of your own thoughts and emotions to better understand and regulate them.

By mastering myself, I unlock my true potential. My inner strength guides me forward.

DAY 117

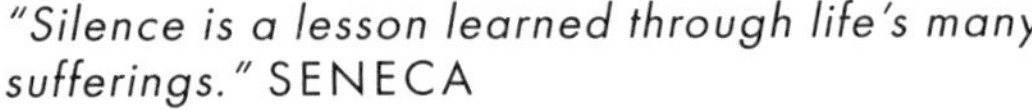

"Silence is a lesson learned through life's many sufferings." SENECA

Silence offers space for reflection, healing and understanding. In a noisy world, embracing quietness allows us to connect with our inner wisdom and find peace. In recovery, moments of silence can be powerful tools for self-discovery and emotional processing.

EMBRACING SILENCE

Create Quiet Time: Dedicate at least 15 minutes today to sit in silence without distractions. Observe your thoughts without judgment.

Listen to the Voice Within: Use this time to tune into your feelings and needs. What is your inner voice telling you?

Practice Mindful Communication: Throughout the day, listen more than you speak. Notice how this affects your interactions.

In silence, I find clarity and peace. I honor the wisdom that arises from stillness.

DAY 118

"To understand the true quality of people, you must look into their minds, and examine their pursuits and aversions." MARCUS AURELIUS

Understanding ourselves deeply requires examining our desires and what we avoid. By owning our motivations and fears, we gain insight into our true nature. In recovery, this self-exploration is crucial for making conscious choices that align with our authentic selves.

DEEP SELF-REFLECTION

Identify Your Pursuits: List activities, goals or possessions you actively seek. Reflect on why they are important to you.

Acknowledge Your Aversions: Note things you avoid or fear. Consider the underlying reasons for these feelings.

Seek Balance: Assess whether your pursuits and aversions serve your well-being. Adjust your focus to align with your core values.

Through honest reflection, I understand myself better. This awareness guides me toward harmony.

DAY 119

Worrying about the future often causes unnecessary suffering. By projecting fears on to events that haven't occurred, we rob ourselves of present peace. In recovery, learning to stay grounded in the present moment reduces anxiety and fosters serenity.

LETTING GO OF WORRIES

Recognize Unproductive Worries: Notice when you're dwelling on future concerns that you cannot control.

Redirect Your Focus: Bring your attention back to the present by engaging in mindful activities or focusing on your immediate surroundings.

Practice Acceptance: Remind yourself that you can handle future challenges as they come. Trust in your resilience and resources.

I release unnecessary worries and embrace the present. I am equipped to face whatever comes my way.

DAY 120

"The more we value things outside our control, the less control we have." EPICTETUS

Placing too much importance on external factors, such as others' opinions, material possessions or uncontrollable events, can lead to instability and disappointment. In recovery, focusing on what we can control—our own thoughts and actions—provides a stable foundation for a lasting change.

FOCUSING ON WHAT YOU CAN CONTROL

List Your Concerns: Write down things that are currently occupying your mind. Categorize them into what you can and cannot control.

Prioritize Your Energy: Commit to investing your time and effort into the areas within your control.

Release the Rest: Practice letting go of concerns beyond your influence. Use affirmations or meditation to reinforce this release.

I focus on what I can control and let go of the rest. This empowers me to live with peace and purpose.

DAY 121

"The soul becomes dyed with the color of its thoughts."
MARCUS AURELIUS

Our thoughts have a profound impact on our inner state and, consequently, our external reality. By nurturing positive, constructive thoughts, we shape a soul that reflects peace, strength and resilience. In recovery, cultivating a healthy mindset is essential for a lasting transformation.

NURTURING POSITIVE THINKING

Monitor Mental Input: Be mindful of the information you consume—books, media, conversations. Choose sources that uplift and inspire you.

Practice Thought Replacement: When negative thoughts arise, consciously replace them with positive alternatives. Affirmations can be a helpful tool for this.

Visualize Positive Outcomes: Spend some time each day imagining positive scenarios and outcomes in your life. This trains your mind to focus on possibilities rather than limitations.

My thoughts shape my reality. I choose thoughts that color my soul with peace and optimism.

DAY 122

"If it is not right, do not do it; if it is not true, do not say it." MARCUS AURELIUS

Integrity is the cornerstone of a virtuous life. Acting rightly and speaking truthfully builds trust with ourselves and others. In recovery, adhering to ethical principles strengthens our character and supports our commitment to change.

PRACTICING INTEGRITY

Reflect on Recent Actions: Consider if there are any actions or words you regret. Acknowledge them without judgment.

Make Amends: If appropriate, take the necessary steps—such as offering an apology or *rectifying a mistake*—to correct any wrongs.

Set Intentions for Honesty: Commit to being truthful in your interactions today, even if it's challenging. Practice expressing yourself with kindness and clarity.

I act with honesty and integrity. My words and actions align with my highest values.

DAY 123

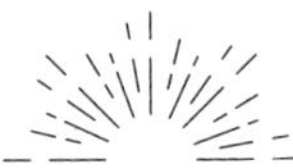

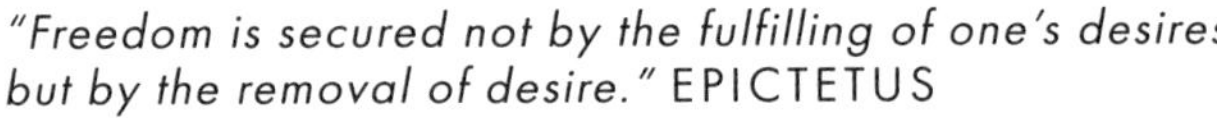

"Freedom is secured not by the fulfilling of one's desires but by the removal of desire." EPICTETUS

Unchecked desires can lead to dissatisfaction and restlessness. By reducing excessive wants, we free ourselves from the constant pursuit of more. In recovery, finding contentment in the present moment enhances our sense of freedom and well-being.

MINIMIZING EXCESSIVE DESIRES

Identify Unnecessary Wants: List material items or experiences you desire that may not contribute to your genuine happiness.

Practice Contentment: Focus on appreciating what you already have. Engage in activities that bring joy without requiring more possessions.

Mindful Consumption: Before making a purchase or pursuing a new desire, pause to consider if it truly serves your well-being.

I am content with what I have. Letting go of excess desires brings me peace and freedom.

DAY 124

"He is a wise man who does not grieve for the things which he has not but rejoices for those which he has."
EPICTETUS

Gratitude shifts our focus from lack to abundance. By appreciating what we have, we cultivate happiness and reduce feelings of envy or dissatisfaction. In recovery, practicing gratitude strengthens our resilience and fosters a positive outlook.

CULTIVATING GRATITUDE

Gratitude List: Write down five things you're grateful for today, no matter how small.

Express Appreciation: Share your gratitude with someone else—thank a friend, a family member or even a stranger who has made a difference in your day.

Mindful Moments: Throughout the day, pause to acknowledge and savor moments of joy or comfort.

My heart is filled with gratitude. I rejoice in the blessings present in my life.

DAY 125

"Do not act as if you were going to live ten thousand years. Death hangs over you. While you live, while it is in your power, be good." MARCUS AURELIUS

Life is fleeting, and tomorrow is not guaranteed. Embracing the impermanence of life can motivate us to live fully and virtuously today. In recovery, this awareness encourages us to prioritize what truly matters and to make each moment count.

LIVING IN THE PRESENT

Acknowledge Mortality: Reflect on the transient nature of life, not to induce fear, but to inspire purposeful living.

Prioritize Meaningful Actions: Identify what is most important to you and dedicate time to these priorities today.

Practice Mindfulness: Engage fully in each activity, giving your complete attention to the present moment.

I embrace the gift of today. I choose to live with purpose, kindness and authenticity.

DAY 126

"Is any man afraid of change? What can take place without change?" MARCUS AURELIUS

Accepting change is the only constant that allows us to adapt more easily to life's fluctuations. Resistance to change can lead to unnecessary suffering. In recovery, flexibility and openness equip us to handle new challenges and opportunities with grace.

ADAPTING TO CHANGE

Identify Recent Changes: Consider changes you've experienced recently, both positive and negative.

Assess Your Response: Reflect on how you've reacted to these changes. Were you resistant or accepting?

Embrace Flexibility: Practice adapting to change with small steps, such as altering your routine or trying a new approach to a task.

I flow with life's changes. Adaptability strengthens me and enriches my journey.

DAY 127

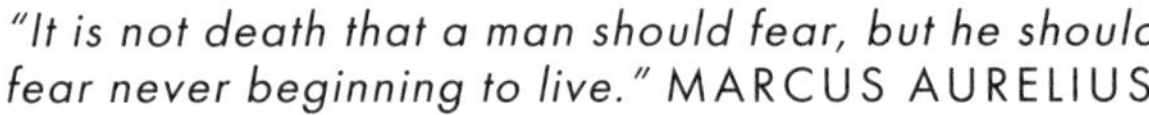

"It is not death that a man should fear, but he should fear never beginning to live." MARCUS AURELIUS

True living involves engaging fully with life, pursuing our passions and connecting deeply with others. Avoiding risks or new experiences out of fear prevents us from truly living. In recovery, stepping out of our comfort zones can lead to profound growth and fulfillment.

EMBRACING LIFE FULLY

Identify What Makes You Feel Alive: What activities, people or passions ignite your spirit? Plan to engage with them regularly.

Overcome a Fear: Choose a fear that has been holding you back and take a step toward confronting it today.

Connect with Others: Reach out to someone you care about or join a community activity to foster meaningful connections.

I choose to live boldly and authentically. I embrace experiences that add value to my life.

DAY 128

"We have two ears and one mouth so that we can listen twice as much as we speak." EPICTETUS

Active listening deepens our understanding and strengthens our relationships. By truly hearing others, we foster empathy and connection. In recovery, listening can provide support and insights that aid our journey.

LISTENING DEEPLY

Engage Fully in Conversations: When speaking with others today, focus entirely on what they're saying without planning your response.

Ask Open-Ended Questions: Encourage others to share more by asking questions that require more than "yes" or "no" answers.

Reflect: Consider their answer before you respond. Find space to show that you understand them and that you're listening.

I listen with an open heart and mind. Through understanding others, I enhance my own perspective.

DAY 129

"Don't explain your philosophy. Embody it."
EPICTETUS

Actions speak louder than words. Living according to our principles is more impactful than merely talking about them. In recovery, embodying our values demonstrates our commitment to change and inspires others by example.

LIVING YOUR PHILOSOPHY

Identify Key Principles: Choose the core principles or values that guide your life.

Align Actions with Principles: Plan specific actions today that reflect these values in tangible ways.

Self-Assessment: At the end of the day, reflect on how well your actions aligned with your philosophy.

I live my values authentically. My life is a reflection of my deepest beliefs.

DAY 130

"The only way to happiness is to cease worrying about things which are beyond the power of our will."
EPICTETUS

Worrying about things outside our control leads to unnecessary stress and detracts from our peace of mind. In recovery, focusing on what we can influence empowers us and enhances our well-being.

LETTING GO OF CONTROL

List Uncontrollable Concerns: Write down worries that are beyond your control.

Acceptance Practice: For each item, acknowledge your inability to change it and affirm your acceptance.

Redirect Focus: Identify areas where you can take positive action and channel your energy there.

I release what I cannot control. My peace comes from focusing on what I can influence.

DAY 131

"If we let things terrify us, life will not be worth living."
SENECA

Fear of the unknown can paralyze us, preventing us from taking meaningful actions. Seneca reminds us that fearing fear—or any inevitable aspect of life—hinders us from fully living. In recovery, embracing life without fear allows us to pursue our passions and make a positive impact.

OVERCOMING FEAR

Identify Your Fears: Write down fears that are limiting your actions or decisions.

Challenge Fearful Thoughts: For each fear, question its validity. What evidence supports it? What might you achieve if you moved past it?

Take Courageous Steps: Choose one small action today that moves you beyond a fear. Celebrate your bravery regardless of the outcome.

I release fear and embrace courage. Living fully means acting despite uncertainty.

DAY 132

"The whole future lies in uncertainty: live immediately."
SENECA

Dwelling on the future can distract us from the richness of the present moment. Seneca advises us to engage with life as it unfolds now. In recovery, being present enhances our appreciation of life and strengthens our resolve.

PRACTICING PRESENCE

Mindful Morning Routine: Start your day with an activity that grounds you in the present, such as meditation, stretching or mindful breathing.

Single-Tasking: Focus on one task at a time today, giving it your full attention without multitasking.

Evening Reflection: At the end of the day, reflect on the moments when you felt truly present. Note how it affected your day.

I live fully in each moment. Embracing the present enriches my life.

DAY 133

"We suffer more often in imagination than in reality."
SENECA

Our minds can create scenarios that amplify fear and anxiety, often out of proportion with reality. Recognizing this tendency helps us distinguish between actual challenges and imagined ones. In recovery, grounding ourselves in reality reduces unnecessary suffering.

DISTINGUISHING REALITY FROM IMAGINATION

Thought Awareness: Notice when you begin worrying or feeling anxious. What are the thoughts that first come to your mind and how do they evolve as you ponder over them?

Reality Check: Observe how your thoughts develop and deepen your fear and anxiety. Assess whether these thoughts are based on facts or assumptions. Seek evidence to support or refute them.

Reframe Your Perspective: Replace exaggerated fears with balanced, rational thoughts.

I focus on what is real and true. Letting go of imagined fears brings me peace.

DAY 134

"To be even-minded is the greatest virtue."
HERACLITUS

Maintaining emotional balance amid life's ups and downs is a hallmark of wisdom. An even mind allows us to respond thoughtfully rather than react impulsively. In recovery, cultivating equanimity supports steady progress and inner calm.

CULTIVATING EQUANIMITY

Emotional Awareness: Throughout the day, check in with your emotions without judgment. Acknowledge what you're feeling.

Balanced Response: When faced with a triggering event, pause before responding. Aim for a measured reaction that reflects your values.

Mindfulness Meditation: Practice a short meditation focusing on your breath to center yourself and promote even-mindedness.

I maintain balance in my heart and mind. Steady and calm, I navigate life's waves.

DAY 135

"No great thing is created suddenly." EPICTETUS

Significant achievements require time, patience and persistent effort. Recognizing this truth helps us set realistic expectations and remain committed. In recovery, acknowledging the gradual nature of healing encourages perseverance.

EMBRACING PATIENCE

Set Realistic Goals: Review your long-term goals and break them into smaller, achievable steps.

Acknowledge Progress: Reflect on how far you've come since beginning your recovery journey. Celebrate milestones, big and small.

Practice Patience: When you feel impatient, remind yourself that a lasting change takes time. Trust the process.

I am patient with myself and my journey. Each day brings me closer to my goals.

DAY 136

"Self-control is strength. Right thought is mastery. Calmness is power." JAMES ALLEN

Inner strength stems from discipline over our impulses, clarity in our thinking and maintaining composure. In recovery, these qualities fortify us against relapse and enhance our ability to handle challenges effectively.

BUILDING INNER STRENGTH

Exercise Self-Control: Identify an area where you can practice restraint today, such as limiting screen time or making healthy food choices.

Cultivate Right Thought: Monitor your thoughts, steering them toward positivity and solutions rather than dwelling on problems.

Maintain Calm: When stress arises, use deep breathing techniques to center yourself before proceeding.

My strength lies within. Through self-control and calm, I can master my life.

DAY 137

"Imagine for yourself a character, a model personality, whose example you determine to follow, in private as well as in public." EPICTETUS

Strong thoughts and emotions are natural and occur within all of us. It's important we recognize this shared humanity in all of us while monitoring our own emotions. In recovery, this balance helps us progress without falling into judgment or resentment.

PRACTICING COMPASSION

Self-Assessment: Identify personal habits or behaviors that reflect your impulsive tendencies. How do you feel about these? Do you wish to change any of these habits or behaviors? Commit to actionable steps toward change.

Exercise Compassion: When others have similar behaviors, choose empathy over criticism. Consider their perspective and challenges.

Model the Behavior: Lead by example, demonstrating the virtues you value through your actions.

I strive for excellence within myself and offer kindness to others. This balance adds meaning to my life.

DAY 138

"It is impossible for a man to learn what he thinks he already knows." EPICTETUS

Open-mindedness is essential for growth. Believing we have nothing more to learn closes us off from new insights and experiences. In recovery, adopting a learner's mindset keeps us receptive to the wisdom that can aid our journey.

EMBRACING A LEARNER'S MINDSET

Identify Areas for Learning: Consider topics or skills you've been resistant to explore. Choose one to investigate.

Seek Knowledge: Engage with books, workshops or conversations that expand your understanding.

Reflect on Learning: At the end of the day, note what you've learned and how it can be applied to your life.

I approach life with curiosity and humility. There is always more to learn.

DAY 139

"First learn the meaning of what you say, and then speak." EPICTETUS

Thoughtful communication strengthens relationships and prevents misunderstandings. By understanding the weight and impact of our words, we can express ourselves more effectively. In recovery, clear and intentional speech fosters trust and connection.

MINDFUL COMMUNICATION

Pause Before Speaking: Before entering conversations, take a moment to consider your words and their potential impact.

Choose Words Wisely: Aim for clarity, honesty and kindness in your speech.

Listen Actively: Focus on understanding others before responding. This enhances mutual respect and understanding.

My words reflect my integrity. I communicate with purpose and care.

DAY 140

"He who is not satisfied with a little is satisfied with nothing." EPICURUS

Contentment doesn't come from abundance but from appreciating what we have. Constant yearning for more leads to perpetual dissatisfaction. In recovery, finding joy in simplicity nurtures inner peace and fulfillment.

APPRECIATING SIMPLICITY

Simplify Your Surroundings: Declutter a space in your home, only keeping items that serve a purpose or bring you joy.

Enjoy Simple Pleasures: Engage in an activity that is uncomplicated yet fulfilling, like a walk in nature or reading a book.

Practice Mindful Gratitude: Throughout the day, pause to appreciate small blessings—early morning sunlight, children laughing in the park, reading your favorite book.

I find joy in simplicity. Contentment fills my heart as I appreciate life's modest gifts.

DAY 141

"Say to yourself ... I shall meet today inquisitive, ungrateful, violent, treacherous, envious, uncharitable men. All these things have come upon them through ignorance of real good and ill." MARCUS AURELIUS

With today's quote, Marcus Aurelius reminds us to prepare ourselves mentally for the challenges we may face each day. By anticipating difficulties, we can approach them with calmness and understanding rather than surprise and frustration. In recovery, being mentally prepared helps us navigate triggers and maintain our composure.

MENTAL PREPARATION FOR THE DAY AHEAD

Morning Reflection: Before starting your day, spend a few minutes considering potential challenges you might encounter.

Set Intentions: Decide how you will respond to difficulties—with patience, empathy or assertiveness.

Affirm Your Strength: Remind yourself of your ability to handle whatever comes your way.

I face each day with readiness and resilience. I am prepared to handle challenges with grace.

DAY 142

"The key is to keep company only with people who uplift you, whose presence calls forth your best."
EPICTETUS

The people we surround ourselves with greatly influence our thoughts and behaviors. Choosing allies who support our growth and well-being is essential. In recovery, fostering positive relationships strengthens our commitment and provides encouragement.

ASSESSING RELATIONSHIPS

Assess Your Circle: Reflect on the people you spend time with. Do they inspire and support you?

Seek Positive Influences: Make an effort to connect with individuals who share your values and uplift you.

Set Boundaries: Gently distance yourself from relationships that hinder your progress or well-being.

I choose relationships that nurture my growth. I am worthy of supportive and positive connections.

DAY 143

"Difficulties strengthen the mind, as labor does the body." SENECA

Just as physical exercise strengthens the body, mental challenges fortify the mind. Embracing difficulties as opportunities for growth enhances our resilience. In recovery, each obstacle we overcome reinforces our mental strength.

EMBRACING MENTAL CHALLENGES

Identify a Challenge: Consider a mental or emotional difficulty you're currently facing.

Develop a Strategy: Plan practical steps to address this challenge, viewing it as a training ground for your mind.

Reflect on Growth: After engaging with the challenge, note how it has contributed to your personal development.

I grow stronger through challenges. My mind is fortified by the trials I overcome.

DAY 144

"The essence of philosophy is that a man should so live that his happiness shall depend as little as possible on external things." EPICTETUS

True happiness arises from within, independent of external circumstances. By cultivating inner peace and contentment, we become less affected by outside events. In recovery, this internal focus empowers us to maintain stability despite life's unpredictability.

CULTIVATING HAPPINESS

Self-Reflection: Identify sources of joy that come from within—personal achievements, virtues or passions.

Mindful Detachment: Practice detaching your happiness from external outcomes or possessions.

Nurture Inner Resources: Engage in activities that enhance your inner well-being, such as cooking your favorite meals, going on leisurely walks, discovering new music or movies.

My happiness is rooted within me. I nurture my inner joy independent of external circumstances.

DAY 145

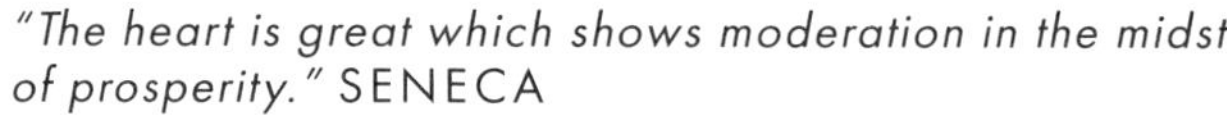

"The heart is great which shows moderation in the midst of prosperity." SENECA

Life ebbs and flows; there are moments of success and moments of failure. In moments of success, we might get carried away by the opulence and grandeur it brings. However, victory is fleeting. By maintaining a strong, humble and virtuous character, especially at our peak, we steer our lives toward continued positive outcomes.

EXERCISING RESTRAINT

Recall Moments of Success: Recall a significant moment in your life where you succeeded at something and describe how you felt at the time. Then, describe how you felt a few days later when the novelty of the success had worn off. Did you do anything, if at all, to hold onto the initial rush of success?

Observations of One Day: Observe one day in your life. You may find several small moments of success and failure. Did you find it difficult to accept the small failures?

Self-Evaluation: Consider two examples—a major life success and a day filled with small successes as well as failures. What do you find similar in your reactions to the two kinds of wins?

Success is transient; when it comes to me, I will accept it with an open heart, and when it leaves me, I will let it go with an open mind.

DAY 146

"Wealth is the slave of a wise man. The master of a fool." SENECA

Wealth, in any form, should serve us rather than control us. When we use resources wisely, they become tools for good. In recovery, maintaining a healthy perspective on material possessions prevents us from becoming enslaved by them.

MANAGING RESOURCES

Assess Your Relationship with Wealth: Reflect on how you view money and possessions. Do they serve your well-being?

Budget Mindfully: Create or review a budget that aligns with your values and goals.

Practice Generosity: Share your resources, whether time, money or skills, to help others.

I control my resources wisely. They serve my highest good and the good of others.

DAY 147

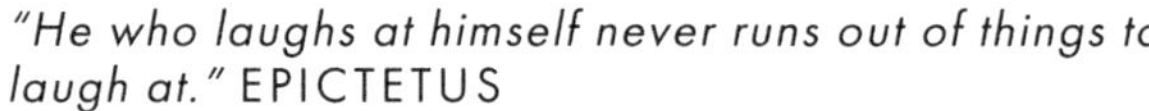

"He who laughs at himself never runs out of things to laugh at." EPICTETUS

Embracing humor about ourselves lightens our spirit and fosters humility. It allows us to accept imperfections and move forward with grace. In recovery, this attitude eases the journey and strengthens resilience.

FINDING JOY IN HUMILITY

Recall a Humorous Moment: Think of a recent mistake or awkward moment and find the humor in it.

Share a Laugh: Connect with someone by sharing a funny story or a joke.

Embrace Imperfection: Accept that making mistakes is part of being human and choose to find joy in them rather than frustration.

I embrace laughter and humility. Joy fills my journey as I accept myself fully.

DAY 148

"Wherever there is a human being, there is an opportunity for a kindness." SENECA

Every interaction is a chance to practice kindness. Small acts can have profound impacts on others and on ourselves. In recovery, cultivating kindness enhances our connections and contributes to a supportive community.

ACTS OF KINDNESS

Perform a Random Act of Kindness: Do something kind for someone without expecting anything in return.

Practice Empathy: Listen attentively to someone who needs to be heard.

Reflect on the Impact: Notice how these acts of kindness affect your mood and perspective.

I choose kindness in all interactions. My actions uplift others and enrich my own spirit.

DAY 149

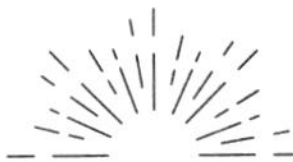

"You are a little soul carrying around a corpse."
EPICTETUS

The above quote is a stark reminder, emphasizing the distinction between our true selves and our physical bodies. Focusing on nurturing our soul—the essence of who we are—brings deeper meaning to life. In recovery, attending to our spiritual well-being is as important as caring for our physical health.

NURTURING THE SOUL

Spiritual Reflection: Spend time engaging in what feeds your soul—nature, art, meditation or service.

Undertake Soulful Activities: Dedicate time today to activities that nourish your inner self.

Mind-Body Connection: Acknowledge your body's role as a vessel and care for it through rest, nutrition and gentle movement.

I honor my soul and care for my body. My inner and outer selves are in harmony.

DAY 150

"The happiness of your life depends upon the quality of your thoughts." MARCUS AURELIUS

Our mindset directly influences our experience of life. By cultivating positive and constructive thoughts, we enhance our happiness. In recovery, managing our thought patterns is key to emotional well-being and sustained progress.

ENHANCING THE QUALITY OF YOUR THOUGHTS

Thought Awareness: Pay attention to recurring thoughts throughout the day. Are they uplifting or draining?

Positive Reframing: When negative thoughts arise, consciously reframe them into positive or neutral ones.

Affirmations: Create personal affirmations that reinforce positive thinking and repeat them regularly.

I cultivate thoughts that bring me joy and peace. My mind is a source of happiness.

DAY 151

"It is not events that disturb people, it is their judgments concerning them." EPICTETUS

Often, it's not the situations themselves that cause us distress, but how we interpret and react to them. By recognizing that our judgments shape our experiences, we can choose perspectives that promote peace and understanding. In recovery, reframing our thoughts empowers us to respond to life's challenges with resilience.

REFRAMING PERSPECTIVES

Identify a Disturbing Event: Think of a recent event that caused you stress or discomfort.

Examine Your Judgment: Reflect on the thoughts and judgments you had about the event. How did they contribute to your distress?

Choose a New Interpretation: Consider alternative ways that are more balanced or positive to view the situation.

I have the power to choose my outlook. By adjusting my judgments, I create a more peaceful inner world.

DAY 152

"He who knows others is wise. He who knows himself is enlightened." LAO TZU

Self-knowledge is the foundation of wisdom. By understanding our thoughts, emotions and motivations, we can navigate life more skillfully. In recovery, deepening our self-awareness helps us identify triggers, recognize patterns and make conscious choices that support our well-being.

GROWING SELF-AWARENESS

Self-Reflection: Spend time journaling about your strengths, weaknesses, desires and fears.

Mindful Observation: Throughout the day, observe your reactions to various situations without judgment.

Seek Feedback: Consider asking trusted friends or mentors for honest feedback to gain additional insights.

I embrace the journey of knowing myself. Self-awareness illuminates my path to growth.

DAY 153

"The obstacle is the way." MARCUS AURELIUS

Challenges are not roadblocks but opportunities for growth. By viewing obstacles as essential parts of our journey, we transform adversity into advantage. In recovery, each hurdle becomes a lesson that strengthens our resolve and advances our progress.

EMBRACING OBSTACLES

Identify Current Obstacles: List any challenges you're currently facing.

Find the Opportunity: For each obstacle, consider what you can learn from it or how it can help you grow.

Take Constructive Action: Decide on a positive step you can take to address or embrace the challenge.

I see obstacles as opportunities. They guide me toward greater strength and wisdom.

DAY 154

"We should always be asking ourselves: 'Is this something that is, or is not, in my control?'" EPICTETUS

Distinguishing between what we can and cannot control allows us to focus our energy effectively. In recovery, accepting what is beyond our control frees us from unnecessary worry, while taking responsibility for what we can influence empowers us.

FOCUSING ON WHAT YOU CAN CONTROL

List Your Concerns: Write down things that are currently on your mind.

Categorize Them: Separate the list into what you can control and what you cannot.

Focus Your Efforts: Commit to taking action on the controllable items and practicing acceptance toward the rest.

I focus on what I can control and let go of what I cannot. This brings me peace and clarity.

DAY 155

"To be content with little is difficult; to be content with much, impossible."
MARIE VON EBNER-ESCHENBACH

Contentment arises not from abundance but from appreciating what we have. Chasing after more can lead to endless dissatisfaction. In recovery, finding joy in simplicity helps us cultivate inner peace and gratitude.

PRACTICING CONTENTMENT

Simplify Your Desires: Reflect on areas where you seek more than necessary.

Appreciate the Present: Make a list of things that fulfill your needs and bring you joy.

Mindful Gratitude: Spend time each day acknowledging and savoring simple pleasures.

I find contentment in simplicity. Appreciating what I have fills me with gratitude.

DAY 156

"Attach yourself to what is spiritually superior, regardless of what other people think or do."
EPICTETUS

Staying true to our values and principles, even when others may not share them, strengthens our character. In recovery, aligning with our higher ideals guides us toward lasting fulfillment and integrity.

ALIGNING WITH YOUR HIGHER IDEALS

Define Your Spiritual Values: Identify the virtues and principles that resonate deeply with you.

Commit to Your Path: Reflect on how you can embody these ideals in your daily life.

Resist External Pressures: Practice standing firm in your values, even when faced with opposition or misunderstanding.

I stay true to my highest values. My commitment to what is right guides my actions.

DAY 157

"Do not indulge in dreams of having what you have not, but reckon up the chief of the blessings you do possess."
MARCUS AURELIUS

Focusing on lack breeds discontent, while appreciating what we have fosters happiness. In recovery, embracing gratitude shifts our mindset from scarcity to abundance, enhancing our overall well-being.

FOSTERING GRATITUDE

Daily Gratitude Practice: Write down three things you're grateful for each day.

Shift Focus from Lack to Abundance: When thoughts of what you lack arise, consciously redirect your attention to your blessings.

Express Appreciation: Share your gratitude with others to strengthen your connections.

My heart overflows with gratitude. I rejoice in the abundance present in my life.

DAY 158

"The happiness of your life depends upon the quality of your thoughts." MARCUS AURELIUS

Our thoughts have a profound impact on our emotions, behaviors and overall well-being. Cultivating a positive and compassionate inner dialogue is essential for a joyful and fulfilling recovery journey.

CULTIVATING POSITIVE SELF-TALK

Notice Your Inner Critic: Pay attention to the way you talk to yourself throughout the day. Is your inner dialogue kind, supportive and encouraging? Or is it critical, judgmental and self-defeating?

Challenge Negative Thoughts: When you notice negative or limiting beliefs, gently question their validity. Are these thoughts based on facts or on old patterns of thinking? What evidence is there to support or refute these thoughts?

Replace with Positive Affirmations: Create a list of affirmations that resonate with you and reflect your desired state of being. Repeat these affirmations to yourself throughout the day, especially when you're feeling challenged.

I choose to focus on positive, life-affirming thoughts that empower me. I am worthy of love, happiness and recovery.

DAY 159

"It is not because things are difficult that we do not dare; it is because we do not dare that they are difficult." SENECA

Fear often magnifies challenges, making them seem insurmountable. By having the courage to face difficulties head-on, we diminish their power over us. In recovery, daring to take bold steps leads to significant breakthroughs.

CULTIVATING COURAGE

Identify a Fear: Choose something you've been avoiding due to fear.

Take a Small Step: Plan and execute a manageable action toward confronting this fear.

Reflect on the Experience: Acknowledge your bravery and consider how facing this fear has changed your perspective.

I dare to face my fears. Courage opens the door to new possibilities.

DAY 160

"The greatest wealth is to live content with little." PLATO

True wealth isn't measured by material possessions but by contentment and peace of mind. In recovery, embracing simplicity and valuing non-material riches leads to lasting fulfillment.

EMBRACING MINIMALISM

Assess Your Possessions: Consider decluttering your environment, keeping only what is useful or brings joy.

Value Experiences over Things: Focus on creating memories and nurturing relationships rather than acquiring more stuff.

Practice Mindful Consumption: Before making new purchases, reflect on whether they truly add value to your life.

I find richness in simplicity. Contentment fills my life with abundance.

DAY 161

"He who conquers himself is the mightiest warrior."
CONFUCIUS

True strength lies not in dominating others but in mastering oneself. By overcoming our inner conflicts and controlling our impulses, we gain the power to navigate life with wisdom and resilience. In recovery, self-mastery leads to a lasting transformation and inner peace.

CULTIVATING SELF-MASTERY

Identify Personal Challenges: Reflect on behaviors or thoughts you'd like to change. What internal battles are you facing?

Set Intentional Goals: Choose one area to focus on and establish clear, achievable objectives.

Practice Consistency: Commit to daily actions that support your goals, acknowledging progress and adjusting as needed.

I am my own master. Through self-discipline and awareness, I achieve true strength.

DAY 162

"The only journey is the one within."
RAINER MARIA RILKE

Our most profound experiences come from exploring our inner world. By turning inward, we gain insights that guide our actions and shape our destiny. In recovery, self-exploration is key to understanding our motivations and healing from within.

THE INWARD JOURNEY

Meditative Reflection: Set aside quiet time to meditate or journal about your thoughts and feelings.

Explore Core Beliefs: Examine the beliefs that influence your behaviors. Are they serving your highest good?

Seek Guidance from Within: Trust your intuition and inner wisdom when making decisions.

My journey inward reveals my true self. I embrace self-discovery with openness and courage.

DAY 163

"We are what we repeatedly do. Excellence, then, is not an act but a habit." WILLIAM DURANT

Our habits define us. By cultivating positive routines and practices, we build a life of excellence. In recovery, establishing healthy habits reinforces our commitment and lays the foundation for sustained well-being.

BUILDING POSITIVE HABITS

Identify Key Habits: Choose habits that support your recovery and personal growth.

Create a Routine: Develop a daily schedule that incorporates these habits, making them a regular part of your life.

Monitor Progress: Keep track of your adherence to these habits, adjusting the plan as necessary to stay on course.

Excellence is my way of life. Through consistent habits, I become the best version of myself.

DAY 164

"Happiness is not something ready-made. It comes from your own actions." DALAI LAMA XIV

True happiness arises from within and is cultivated through our choices and actions. By engaging in activities that align with our values and bring joy, we create our own happiness. In recovery, proactive efforts toward our well-being enhance our sense of fulfillment.

CREATING YOUR HAPPINESS

Engage in Joyful Activities: Identify activities that bring you genuine happiness and schedule time for them.

Act with Kindness: Perform acts of kindness for others, boosting both their happiness and your own.

Reflect on Positive Actions: At the end of the day, acknowledge the actions you took that contributed to your happiness.

I create my own happiness through my actions. Joy is a product of my choices.

DAY 165

"The greater the difficulty, the more glory in surmounting it." EPICTETUS

Overcoming significant challenges brings a profound sense of accomplishment. Difficulties test our limits and strengthen our character. In recovery, facing and surmounting obstacles reinforces our resilience and commitment.

EMBRACING CHALLENGES

Acknowledge Difficulties: Recognize the challenges you're currently facing without minimizing them.

Formulate a Plan: Develop a strategy to address these challenges, breaking them into manageable steps.

Celebrate Victories: Honor your progress and success, no matter how small.

I rise to meet challenges with courage. Overcoming them brings strength and honor.

DAY 166

"You have within you right now, everything you need to deal with whatever the world can throw at you."
BRIAN TRACY

We possess innate strength and resources to face life's adversities. Trusting in our capabilities empowers us to handle any situation. In recovery, believing in ourselves is crucial for overcoming obstacles and maintaining progress.

TRUSTING YOUR INNER RESOURCES

Recall Past Successes: Reflect on times when you overcame difficulties, noting the strengths you utilized.

Affirm Your Abilities: Remind yourself of your skills, talents and qualities that enable you to handle challenges.

Face the Day with Confidence: Approach today's tasks with the assurance that you are capable and prepared.

I have all I need within me. My inner strength guides me through any challenges I may face.

DAY 167

"The art of living is more like wrestling than dancing, in so far as it stands ready against the accidental and the unforeseen, and is not apt to fall" MARCUS AURELIUS

Life often requires effort, resilience and adaptability. Embracing life's struggles as part of the journey helps us develop fortitude. In recovery, recognizing that challenges are opportunities to strengthen ourselves fosters perseverance.

BUILDING RESILIENCE

Anticipate Challenges: Accept that difficulties are a natural part of life and prepare mentally.

Build Coping Skills: Identify and practice strategies that help you manage stress effectively.

Stay Adaptable: Maintain flexibility and be willing to adjust your approach as situations change.

I grapple with life's challenges bravely. Each struggle hones my strength and resilience.

DAY 168

"He who is contented is rich." LAO TZU

True wealth is found in contentment, not material abundance. By appreciating what we have, we experience a richness that external possessions cannot provide. In recovery, cultivating contentment enhances our satisfaction with life.

PURSUING CONTENTMENT

Practice Mindful Gratitude: Spend time appreciating the simple things in your life.

Limit Comparisons: Avoid comparing yourself to others, focusing instead on your own journey.

Simplify Desires: Recognize when desires lead to dissatisfaction and refocus on what truly matters.

I am rich in contentment. Appreciating what I have brings me lasting fulfillment.

DAY 169

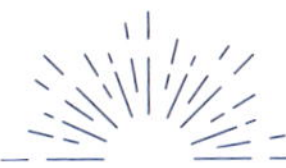

"Knowing yourself is the beginning of all wisdom."
ARISTOTLE

Self-knowledge lays the groundwork for personal growth and wise decision-making. Understanding our strengths, weaknesses and motivations allows us to navigate life more effectively. In recovery, self-awareness is vital for recognizing triggers and fostering healing.

FOSTERING SELF-KNOWLEDGE

Personal Inventory: Assess your values, beliefs and goals. How do they align with your current actions?

Acknowledge Emotions: Pay attention to your feelings throughout the day, taking note of what triggers certain emotions.

Reflect on the Past: Consider how past experiences have shaped who you are today, and analyze how you can use this knowledge in your journey forward.

I seek to know myself deeply. Self-understanding guides me toward wisdom.

DAY 170

"If one does not know to which port one is sailing, no wind is favorable." SENECA

Having clear goals and direction gives purpose to our actions. Without a destination in mind, we can drift aimlessly. In recovery, setting meaningful objectives helps us stay focused and motivated.

DEFINING YOUR DIRECTION

Set Clear Goals: Identify short-term and long-term goals that inspire and challenge you.

Create an Action Plan: Outline steps needed to achieve these goals, making them specific and attainable.

Monitor Progress: Regularly review your goals and adjust your plans as necessary to stay on course.

I chart my course with purpose. Clear goals guide me toward my desired destination.

DAY 171

"He who fears he shall suffer, already suffers what he fears." MICHEL DE MONTAIGNE

Worrying about potential future suffering causes us to experience that suffering prematurely. By focusing on the present moment and letting go of fear, we can reduce unnecessary stress. In recovery, moving away from unnecessary fear allows us to embrace peace and confidence in our journey.

LETTING GO OF FEAR

Identify Fears: Write down any fears that are causing you anxiety or holding you back.

Challenge Fearful Thoughts: Question the likelihood of these fears coming true. Are they based on evidence or assumptions?

Focus on the Present: Engage in mindfulness practices to anchor yourself in the present moment, reducing the power of fear over you.

I release fear and embrace the present. I am capable of handling whatever comes my way.

DAY 172

"Don't explain your philosophy. Embody it."
EPICTETUS

Often, it might seem easier to engage with the intellectual aspects of recovery—reading books, attending meetings and talking about our progress. However, true transformation occurs when we put these principles into practice, allowing our actions to speak louder than words.

ALIGNING ACTIONS WITH YOUR VALUES

Identify a Value to Focus On: From your list of core values, choose one to emphasize today. This might be honesty, compassion, courage or any quality that resonates with you.

Look for Opportunities: Throughout your day, be mindful of how you can embody this value in your interactions, decisions and responses.

Reflect at the End of the Day: Before bed, take a few moments to reflect on your day. How well did you align your actions with your chosen value? What did you learn?

I am committed to living a life of integrity where my actions consistently reflect my values. I embrace each opportunity to grow.

DAY 173

"It is possible to curb your arrogance, to overcome pleasure and pain, to rise above your ambition and to not be angry with stupid and ungrateful people—yes, even to care for them." MARCUS AURELIUS

Responding to harm with harm only perpetuates negativity. By choosing to act with integrity and kindness, we break this cycle and maintain our own peace. In recovery, this approach helps us heal relationships and foster a positive environment.

ACTING WITH INTEGRITY

Reflect on Grievances: Consider any resentment or grudge you may be holding on to.

Choose Your Response: Decide how you can respond in a way that aligns with your values, rather than reacting impulsively.

Practice Forgiveness: Work on letting go of anger and forgiving others, not for their sake, but to free yourself from negativity.

I choose to act with integrity. I release negativity and embrace peace.

DAY 174

"Be tolerant with others and strict with yourself."
MARCUS AURELIUS

Holding ourselves accountable while extending understanding to others fosters personal growth and harmonious relationships. In recovery, this balance helps us improve ourselves without feeling the need to judge others.

BALANCING COMPASSION AND ACCOUNTABILITY

Self-Assessment: Identify areas where you can improve and set specific goals for personal development.

Practice Empathy: When others make mistakes, strive to understand their perspective and refrain from harsh judgment.

Lead by Example: Demonstrate the virtues you value through your actions, inspiring others through your conduct.

I hold myself to high standards and offer compassion to others. Through this, I grow and contribute positively to the world.

DAY 175

"If you are distressed by anything external, the pain is not due to the thing itself but to your estimate of it; and this you have the power to revoke at any moment."
MARCUS AURELIUS

Our perception of events determines our emotional responses. By reframing our thoughts, we can reduce distress and regain control over our reactions. In recovery, this empowers us to navigate challenges with equanimity.

REFRAMING PERCEPTIONS

Identify a Stressor: Think of a recent event that caused you distress.

Examine Your Interpretation: Reflect on how your perception contributed to your emotional response.

Choose a New Perspective: Reframe the situation in a more positive or neutral light, focusing on what you can learn or how you can grow from it.

I have the power to choose my response. I view challenges as opportunities for growth.

DAY 176

"We suffer more often in imagination than in reality."
SENECA

Our minds can create scenarios that cause unnecessary anxiety. By staying grounded in reality, we can alleviate imagined suffering. In recovery, focusing on the present moment helps us maintain peace of mind.

GROUNDING YOURSELF IN REALITY

Notice Worrying Thoughts: Pay close attention to moments when certain actions or events cause you to worry about future events or dwell on the past.

Assess the Reality: Check whether your anxious thoughts impact your objective understanding of the said situations causing you distress. Ask yourself if these thoughts are based on facts or assumptions.

Engage in Mindfulness: Practice mindfulness exercises to bring your attention back to the present.

I release unnecessary worries. I focus on the present and trust in my ability to handle whatever comes.

DAY 177

"Luck is what happens when preparation meets opportunity." SENECA

We create our own luck through diligent preparation and openness to opportunities. In recovery, consistently working on ourselves positions us to seize positive opportunities when they arise.

PREPARING FOR SUCCESS

Set Clear Goals: Identify your personal and recovery-related goals.

Develop a Plan: Outline the steps you need to take to prepare yourself for opportunities that would align with your goals.

Stay Open: Cultivate an open mind to recognize and embrace opportunities when they appear.

I prepare diligently and remain open to possibilities. I create my own luck.

DAY 178

"The soul becomes dyed with the color of its thoughts."
MARCUS AURELIUS

Our thoughts deeply influence our character and emotions. By nurturing positive and virtuous thoughts, we cultivate a healthy and equanimous soul. In recovery, this practice supports a lasting positive inner transformation.

NURTURING VIRTUOUS THOUGHTS

Foster Awareness: Observe your thoughts throughout the day without judgment.

Cultivate Positivity: Intentionally focus on thoughts of kindness, gratitude and compassion.

Limit Negative Influences: Reduce exposure to negative media or environments that may affect your thoughts adversely.

My thoughts shape my soul. I choose thoughts that bring peace and positivity.

DAY 179

"Do not act as if you were going to live ten thousand years. Death hangs over you. While you live, while it is in your power, be good." MARCUS AURELIUS

Our time is precious, and life is transient. Accepting this motivates us to be aware, live purposefully and make meaningful contributions. In recovery, focusing on purposeful living enriches our journey and impacts those around us.

LIVING PURPOSEFULLY

Reflect on Your Purpose: Consider what gives your life meaning and how you can contribute positively to the world.

Take Action Today: Identify one action you can take today that aligns with your purpose or values.

Practice Being Present: Engage fully in each moment, appreciating the gift of today.

I live with purpose and intention.
I make the most of each day.

DAY 180

"How long are you going to wait before you demand the best for yourself?" EPICTETUS

We often postpone pursuing our highest potential, settling for less than we deserve. By committing to our own growth and well-being, we honor ourselves and our journey. In recovery, demanding the best for ourselves propels us toward healing and fulfillment.

COMMITTING TO GROWTH

Identify Areas for Growth: Reflect on aspects of your life where you can strive for better.

Set High Standards: Establish goals that challenge you to reach your full potential.

Take Immediate Action: Begin today with one step, no matter how small, toward demanding the best for yourself.

I deserve the best and commit to pursuing it. My growth begins now.

DAY 181

"The happiness of your life depends upon the quality of your thoughts." MARCUS AURELIUS

Our inner dialogues profoundly influence our emotions and actions. By nurturing positive and constructive thoughts, we create a foundation for a fulfilling life. In recovery, mindfully choosing our thoughts empowers us to overcome challenges and embrace joy.

CULTIVATING POSITIVE THOUGHTS

Monitor Your Inner Dialogues: Pay attention to your self-talk throughout the day. Note when negative thoughts arise.

Reframe Negative Thoughts: When you catch a negative thought, challenge it and rephrase it positively or realistically.

Practice Gratitude: Begin or end your day by listing things you're grateful for, reinforcing a positive mindset.

I fill my mind with thoughts that uplift and inspire me. My positive mindset shapes my reality.

DAY 182

"If I didn't define myself for myself, I would be crunched into other people's fantasies for me and eaten alive."
AUDRE LORDE

Clarity about who we want to become guides our actions and decisions. By envisioning our ideal self, we set a direction for our journey. In recovery, this vision motivates us to make choices that align with our highest aspirations.

DEFINING YOUR IDEAL SELF

Visualize Your Future Self: Spend time imagining yourself as the person you aspire to be. What qualities do you embody?

Set Aligned Goals: Identify specific actions that will move you toward becoming this person.

Take Consistent Steps: Commit to daily practices that reinforce these qualities and bring your vision to life.

I am becoming the person I aspire to be. Each action I take aligns with my highest self.

DAY 183

"You have power over your mind—not outside events. Realize this, and you will find strength."
MARCUS AURELIUS

Focusing on controlling our internal world rather than external circumstances empowers us. In recovery, directing our energy toward managing our thoughts and reactions enhances our resilience and peace.

STRENGTHENING INNER CONTROL

Identify External Stressors: List things outside your control that are causing you concern.

Shift Focus Inward: For each stressor, consider how you can adjust your mindset or response.

Practice Acceptance: Embrace what you cannot change and focus on influencing what you can—your own actions and attitudes.

I focus on my inner world, where my true power lies. I find strength in managing my mind.

DAY 184

"He who lives in harmony with himself lives in harmony with the universe." MARCUS AURELIUS

Inner harmony arises from self-acceptance and aligning our actions with our values. In recovery, fostering peace within ourselves reflects outward, improving our relationships and overall well-being.

CULTIVATING HARMONY

Self-Compassion: Practice forgiving yourself for past mistakes and acknowledge your progress.

Align Actions with Values: Ensure your daily actions reflect your core beliefs and principles.

Mindful Living: Engage in activities that promote balance and well-being, such as meditation or nature walks.

I nurture peace within myself. Living authentically brings me harmony and fulfillment.

DAY 185

"The greater the obstacle, the more glory in overcoming it."
MOLIÈRE

Challenges test our strength and character. Overcoming significant obstacles enhances our confidence and sense of achievement. In recovery, each hurdle surmounted is a testament to our resilience.

EMBRACING CHALLENGES

Identify a Current Obstacle: Reflect on a significant challenge you're facing at the moment.

Plan Your Approach: Break down the steps needed to overcome this obstacle.

Seek Support: Reach out to friends, mentors or support groups for guidance and encouragement.

I face challenges with courage. Overcoming obstacles strengthens me.

DAY 186

"Fortify yourself with contentment, for this is an impregnable fortress." EPICTETUS

Happiness is not dependent on external factors but on our mindset. By cultivating gratitude and focusing on the positives, we can create a fulfilling life. In recovery, this shift in perspective supports sustained joy.

FOSTERING INNER JOY

Daily Gratitude: Note at least three things you're grateful for today.

Positive Affirmations: Create statements that promote self-love and optimism, and repeat them to yourself whenever necessary.

Mindful Presence: Engage fully in the present moment, appreciating simple pleasures.

Happiness resides within me. I choose thoughts that bring joy and contentment.

DAY 187

"If you seek tranquility, do less." MARCUS AURELIUS

Simplifying our lives reduces stress and creates space for peace. By focusing on what truly matters, we enhance our well-being. In recovery, prioritizing essential activities supports a balanced lifestyle.

SIMPLIFYING YOUR LIFE

Assess Commitments: Review your schedule and identify non-essential tasks you can eliminate.

Prioritize Self-Care: Allocate time for rest, reflection and activities that nourish your soul.

Practice Saying No: Set healthy boundaries by respectfully declining additional obligations that overwhelm you.

I simplify my life to cultivate peace. Tranquility grows as I focus on what truly matters.

DAY 188

"The only true wisdom is in knowing you know nothing."
SOCRATES

We often enter recovery with preconceived notions, judgments and expectations about ourselves and the journey ahead. Socrates's words encourage us to approach this process with humility, curiosity and a willingness to learn and grow. Let go of the need to have all the answers and embrace the transformative power of a beginner's mind.

APPROACHING RECOVERY WITH A BEGINNER'S MIND

Release Expectations: What assumptions or expectations have you been holding on to about recovery? Gently release any rigid ideas about what this journey *should* look like and open yourself to new possibilities.

Cultivate Curiosity: Approach each day as a chance to learn something new about yourself, your triggers and the tools that support your well-being.

Practice Non-Judgment: Treat yourself with the same kindness and compassion you would offer a friend who is learning something new. Mistakes are inevitable, but each experience offers an opportunity for growth.

I release the need to be perfect and embrace the journey of recovery with an open mind and a willing heart.

DAY 189

"He who laughs at himself never runs out of things to laugh at." EPICTETUS

Embracing humility and finding humor in our imperfections lightens our spirit. It fosters resilience and joy. In recovery, this attitude helps us navigate setbacks with grace.

STAYING LIGHTHEARTED

Reflect on a Silly Moment: Recall a recent situation where you found an opportunity to laugh at yourself.

Share Laughter: Connect with a friend or loved one and exchange such humorous stories about yourselves.

Release Perfectionism: Accept that making mistakes is a part of growth and choose to find joy in the journey.

I embrace humor and humility. Laughing at myself brings joy and eases my path.

DAY 190

"The best answer to anger is silence."
MARCUS AURELIUS

Anger is like a roaring fire, and when it is lit, it can consume us. While it is a natural emotion that is essential to express, we must know when to express our anger and how to respond to another's anger. In recovery, learn how to be calm in the face of your own, as well as another's anger.

MANAGING ANGER

Observe Angry Behaviors: Think of the last time you felt truly angry. How did the situation arise and how did you respond?

Reflect on Actions: How did your actions affect those around you? Did they respond with anger, silence or something in between? How did those heightened emotions affect the situation at hand?

Identify Consequences and Determine Solutions: Consider what the triggers were and how these feelings developed in your mind and heart. Contemplate how you felt the anger gradually building up inside you and explore healthier ways to channel this energy.

I will express my emotions in a healthy manner that is fulfilling without being destructive or hurtful.

DAY 191

"Waste no more time arguing what a good person should be. Be one." MARCUS AURELIUS

Instead of debating or examining what it means to be good, embody those qualities through your actions. In recovery, leading by example not only reinforces your own commitment but also inspires others.

LIVING YOUR VALUES

Identify Core Values: List the virtues that are most important to you, such as honesty, compassion or courage.

Align Actions with Values: Reflect on how your daily actions can embody these virtues. Set specific intentions to align your actions with your values today.

Self-Reflection: At the end of the day, assess how well you embodied your values and consider areas for improvement.

I choose to live my values authentically. My actions reflect the goodness I seek.

DAY 192

"You could leave life right now. Let that determine what you do and say and think." MARCUS AURELIUS

Life is unpredictable, and time is precious. Let this awareness motivate you to live fully and intentionally. In recovery, seizing each moment reinforces the value of your journey.

EMBRACING THE PRESENT

Mindful Morning: Begin your day by acknowledging the gift of life and setting an intention to make the most of it.

Engage Fully: Be present in your activities, giving your full attention to each task and interaction.

Express Appreciation: Share gratitude and love with those around you to strengthen your connections.

I live each moment with purpose and gratitude. My actions today reflect my values of life.

DAY 193

"No man is free who is not master of himself."
EPICTETUS

True freedom comes from self-control and mastery over one's desires and impulses. In recovery, developing self-discipline empowers you to make choices that align with your true self.

BUILDING SELF-DISCIPLINE

Set Personal Rules: Define guidelines for yourself that support your well-being and recovery.

Practice Mindfulness: Stay aware of temptations or triggers and employ strategies to manage them effectively.

Reward Progress: Acknowledge and celebrate your efforts in exercising self-control.

I am the master of my actions and choices. Through self-discipline, I achieve true freedom.

DAY 194

"It is not what happens to you but how you react to it that matters." EPICTETUS

External events are often beyond our control, but our responses are within our power. In recovery, choosing constructive reactions fosters resilience and personal growth.

MANAGING REACTIONS

Pause Before Responding: When faced with a challenging situation, take a moment to breathe and collect your thoughts.

Choose Your Response: Consider responses that align with your values and support your well-being.

Reflect on Outcomes: Afterward, evaluate how your chosen reaction affected the situation and your emotions.

I control my reactions. By responding thoughtfully, I shape my experience positively.

DAY 195

"Receive the gifts of fortune without pride; and part with them without reluctance." MARCUS AURELIUS

Embracing humility opens the door to learning and growth. In recovery, acknowledging that there's always more to understand keeps you receptive to new insights and support.

CULTIVATING HUMILITY

Adopt a Learner's Mindset: Approach each day as an opportunity to learn something new.

Seek Feedback: Be open to constructive criticism and consider how it can aid your development.

Practice Active Listening: Give full attention to others when they speak, valuing their perspectives.

I embrace humility and remain open to learning. Wisdom grows as I acknowledge what I do not know.

DAY 196

"To improve is to change; to be perfect is to change often." WINSTON CHURCHILL

Continuous improvement requires flexibility and a willingness to adapt. In recovery, embracing change is essential for personal evolution and overcoming challenges.

EMBRACING CHANGE

Identify Areas for Change: Reflect on habits or beliefs that may be hindering your progress.

Set Goals: Establish clear, achievable objectives to make the necessary changes.

Adapt and Evolve: Monitor your progress and be willing to adjust your approach as needed.

I welcome change as a pathway to growth. Each adjustment brings me closer to my best self.

DAY 197

"Be kind, for everyone you meet is fighting a hard battle." PLATO

Recognizing that others face their own struggles as well fosters empathy and compassion. In recovery, extending kindness strengthens your connections and enriches your own spirit.

PRACTICING EMPATHY

Mindful Interactions: Approach others with patience and understanding, even in difficult situations.

Offer Support: Provide a listening ear or a helping hand to someone who may be struggling.

Reflect on Shared Humanity: Acknowledge the common challenges we all face and let this awareness guide your actions.

I choose kindness and empathy. My compassion uplifts others and nourishes my soul.

DAY 198

"Silence is a source of great strength." LAO TZU

Embracing silence allows for introspection and rejuvenation. In recovery, taking time for quiet reflection strengthens your inner resolve and clarity.

EMBRACING SILENCE

Schedule Quiet Time: Dedicate a portion of your day to unplug from distractions and sit in silence.

Practice Mindfulness Meditation: Focus on your breath and observe your thoughts without judgment.

Listen to Your Inner Voice: Use this time to connect with your deeper self and your intuition.

In silence, I find strength and clarity. Quiet moments restore my spirit.

DAY 199

"I begin to speak only when I'm certain what I'll say isn't better left unsaid" CATO THE YOUNGER

Wisdom often comes with humility and the understanding that actions speak louder than words. In recovery, focusing on personal growth rather than boasting about it leads to genuine progress.

VALUING ACTIONS OVER WORDS

Reflect Before Speaking: Consider the impact of your words and whether it is necessary for you to speak in this situation before you share your thoughts.

Demonstrate Through Actions: Let your behaviors and choices reflect your commitments and values.

Practice Humility: Acknowledge that there is always more to learn and understand.

I let my actions speak for me. Through my humility and my deeds, I embody my principles.

DAY 200

"The journey of a thousand miles begins with a single step." LAO TZU

Every significant endeavor starts with a simple action. In recovery, acknowledging the progress you've made reinforces the importance of each step taken along your journey.

RECOGNIZING YOUR PROGRESS

Celebrate Milestones: Reflect on how far you've come since you began your recovery.

Set Future Goals: Identify new objectives to continue your progress in the days ahead.

Stay Committed: Renew your dedication to taking consistent steps forward.

Every step I take matters. I honor my journey and look forward to the path ahead.

DAY 201

"Your ability to control your thoughts—treat it with respect. It's all that protects your mind from false perceptions—false to your nature, and that of all rational beings." MARCUS AURELIUS

Our perceptions shape our reality, but we can reason with perceptions and rationalize them. Events themselves are neutral; it's our interpretation that assigns them meaning. In recovery, recognizing that we have control over our interpretations empowers us to choose perspectives that support our well-being.

SHIFTING PERCEPTIONS

Identify a Disturbing Event: Think of a recent situation that upset you.

Examine Your Interpretation: Analyze how your perception influenced your emotional response.

Choose a Positive Perspective: Look at the event through a positive lens, and reframe it as an opportunity to learn a new lesson and grow.

I have the power to choose my perceptions. By adjusting my views, I cultivate peace and resilience.

DAY 202

"The greater part of our happiness or misery depends upon our dispositions and not upon our circumstances."
MARTHA WASHINGTON

Our inner attitude significantly influences our experience of life. By cultivating a positive disposition, we can find contentment regardless of external situations. In recovery, focusing on our mindset enhances our ability to navigate challenges.

CULTIVATING A POSITIVE DISPOSITION

Morning Affirmations: Begin your day with positive statements about yourself and your life.

Practice Gratitude: Throughout the day, acknowledge and appreciate the things you feel blessed to have.

Spread Positivity: Offer kind words or gestures to others. This will not only enhance their mood but yours as well.

My happiness depends on my attitude. I choose positivity and gratitude.

DAY 203

"The impediment to action advances action. What stands in the way becomes the way."
MARCUS AURELIUS

Obstacles are not just barriers; they can become the path forward. Each challenge offers lessons that propel us ahead. In recovery, embracing difficulties transforms them into stepping stones toward growth.

EMBRACING OBSTACLES

Identify Current Challenges: Write down the obstacles you're facing right now.

Find the Lesson: For each obstacle consider what you can learn from it or how it can help you improve.

Take Action: Develop a step-by-step plan to address the obstacle, turning it into an opportunity.

Obstacles become my path. I grow stronger with each challenge I embrace.

DAY 204

"He who angers you conquers you."
ELIZABETH KENNY

By allowing others to provoke us, we relinquish our power; however, by maintaining composure, we stay in control of ourselves. In recovery, mastering our emotions protects our peace and progress.

MAINTAINING EMOTIONAL CONTROL

Recognize Triggers: Take note of situations or people that tend to upset you.

Develop Coping Strategies: Practice techniques like deep breathing or prepare positive affirmations to use when triggered.

Reflect on Responses: After unpleasant encounters, assess how you managed your emotions and how you might improve in the future.

I control my emotions. I remain calm and composed, preserving my inner peace.

DAY 205

"The best way to predict the future is to create it."
ABRAHAM LINCOLN

We have the power to shape our destiny through our actions today. By setting intentions and taking steps toward our goals, we actively create our future. In recovery, proactive effort leads to a lasting change.

CREATING YOUR FUTURE

Define Your Vision: Reflect on what you want your future to look like.

Set Goals: Establish clear, achievable objectives that will lead you toward your vision.

Take Daily Actions: Commit to taking small steps each day that contribute toward your long-term goals.

I am the architect of my future. My actions today build the life I desire.

DAY 206

"An ounce of prevention is worth a pound of cure."
BENJAMIN FRANKLIN

Addressing potential issues before they become problems saves us from greater hardships later. In recovery, implementing preventative measures strengthens our resilience against relapse.

GUARDING THE MIND

Identify Risks: Consider situations or behaviors that may jeopardize your recovery.

Develop Strategies: Create plans to avoid or manage these risks effectively.

Maintain Healthy Habits: Engage in routines that support your physical and mental well-being.

I take proactive steps to protect my well-being. Prevention strengthens my journey.

DAY 207

"Happiness depends upon ourselves." ARISTOTLE

We are responsible for our own happiness. We cultivate joy by choosing thoughts and actions that align with our values. This empowers us to create a fulfilling life while on our recovery journey.

TAKING RESPONSIBILITY FOR YOUR HAPPINESS

Self-Care Activities: Plan activities that bring you joy and relaxation.

Positive Relationships: Surround yourself with people who uplift and support you.

Mindset Shift: Replace limiting beliefs with empowering thoughts.

My happiness is my responsibility. I choose actions and thoughts that bring me joy.

DAY 208

"He who has a why to live for can bear almost any how." FRIEDRICH NIETZSCHE

A strong sense of purpose helps us endure hardships. Knowing our "why" provides motivation and direction. In recovery, clarifying our purpose fuels perseverance.

SEEKING PURPOSE

Reflect on Passions: Identify what activities or causes ignite your enthusiasm.

Define Your Purpose: Articulate a personal mission statement that captures your "why."

Align Actions: Ensure your daily activities support and reflect your purpose.

My purpose guides me. Having a clear "why" allows me to navigate life's challenges with strength.

DAY 209

"No one can make you feel inferior without your consent." ELEANOR ROOSEVELT

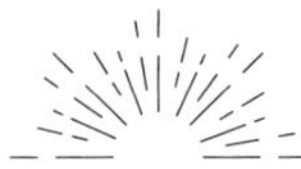

Our self-worth is determined by us, not others. Refusing to internalize negative opinions protects our confidence. In recovery, maintaining self-esteem is vital for progress.

AFFIRMING SELF-WORTH

Recognize Negative Influences: Identify sources that make you feel diminished.

Set Boundaries: Limit exposure to these influences and assert your needs respectfully.

Practice Self-affirmation: Regularly remind yourself of your strengths and inherent value.

I define my worth. I honor and respect myself, independent of others' opinions.

DAY 210

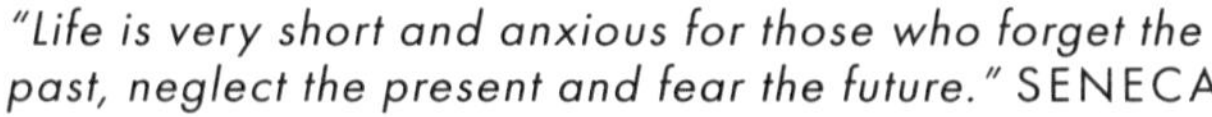

"Life is very short and anxious for those who forget the past, neglect the present and fear the future." SENECA

Being present allows us to fully experience life without the burdens of past regrets or future anxieties. In recovery, embracing the present moment enhances our appreciation and reduces stress.

LIVING IN THE PRESENT

Mindfulness Meditation: Spend time focusing on your breath and sensations to ground yourself in the now.

Let Go of Regrets: Acknowledge past mistakes, learn from them and release them.

Release Worry: Accept that the future is uncertain and choose to focus on what you can do today.

I embrace the present moment. Living fully now brings peace and fulfillment.

DAY 211

"Do not let the behavior of others destroy your inner peace." DALAI LAMA

Maintaining inner peace is essential for well-being. In allowing others' actions to disturb us, we lose our power. In recovery, safeguarding our serenity helps us stay grounded and focused on our journey.

PRESERVING INNER PEACE

Set Boundaries: Recognize when someone's behavior is affecting you negatively and establish healthy limits.

Practice Detachment: Understand that others' actions are a reflection of them, not you. Choose not to take things personally.

Center Yourself: Use techniques like deep breathing and engage in mindful activities to reconnect with your calm center when feeling disturbed.

I protect my inner peace. Others' actions do not disturb my tranquility.

DAY 212

"To understand the world, you must first understand yourself."
SOCRATES

Self-awareness is the key to understanding our place in the world. By delving into our thoughts, emotions and behaviors, we gain clarity that enhances our interactions with others. In recovery, self-understanding is foundational for a lasting change.

BECOMING SELF-AWARE

Self-Reflection: Spend time journaling about your feelings, thoughts and reactions.

Identify Patterns: Notice recurring themes or triggers in your behavior.

Seek Insight: Consider speaking with a counselor, mentor or a trusted friend to gain additional perspectives.

I explore my inner world with honesty. Self-understanding illuminates my path.

DAY 213

"It's not what happens to you but how you react to it that matters." EPICTETUS

Life is unpredictable, but our reactions are within our control. By choosing constructive responses, we shape our experiences positively. In recovery, mastering our reactions is crucial for overcoming challenges.

MINDFUL RESPONSES

Pause and Breathe: When faced with a stimulus, take a moment to breathe before reacting.

Consider the Outcome: Reflect on how different responses may affect the situation and your well-being.

Choose Wisely: Opt for the response that aligns with your values and supports your recovery.

I control my reactions. I respond thoughtfully and align my actions with my values.

DAY 214

"Be yourself; everyone else is already taken."
OSCAR WILDE

Authenticity is liberating. Embracing who we truly are allows us to live honestly and build genuine connections. In recovery, being authentic strengthens our self-esteem and integrity.

EMBRACING AUTHENTICITY

Acknowledge Your Truths: Reflect on your beliefs, values and desires without judgment.

Express Yourself: Find ways to share your authentic self with others, whether through conversation, art or other forms of expression.

Let Go of Comparison: Release the urge to compare yourself to others; focus on your unique journey.

I embrace my true self. Authenticity brings me freedom and fulfillment.

DAY 215

"Freedom isn't secured by filling up on your heart's desire but by removing your desire." EPICTETUS

Freedom is true wealth, as are contentment and simplicity. By reducing unnecessary desires, we experience greater satisfaction with what we have. In recovery, this mindset helps us appreciate life's true riches.

BUILDING CONTENTMENT

Evaluate Desires: Identify your wants. Divide them into health, spiritual and material. Note how important these are to you and what you will do to achieve them.

Examine Your Actions: Reflect on the actions that you are taking to achieve your wants. Are they taking away from other important ventures and parts of your life?

Finding Freedom: If you had to drop a particular material want from your life—completely cease all thoughts and actions related to it—what would you gain back? Reflect on what this means for your peace of mind.

I am content with all that I have and that makes me free.

DAY 216

"He who laughs at himself never runs out of things to laugh at." EPICTETUS

Maintaining a sense of humor about ourselves lightens burdens and fosters resilience. In recovery, this attitude helps us navigate setbacks with grace and optimism.

EMBRACING THE SELF

Reflect on Lighthearted Moments: Recall times when you laughed at your own mistakes and how it helped you move forward.

Share a Laugh: Connect with someone by sharing a funny personal story. Ask them about similar experiences they might have had.

Embrace Imperfection: Recognize that making mistakes is human; choose to see them as opportunities for growth.

I laugh with myself, not at myself. Joy and self-acceptance brighten my journey.

DAY 217

"Do every act of your life as though it were the very last act of your life." MARCUS AURELIUS

Approaching each action with full presence and intention enhances the quality of our lives. This focus helps us make meaningful choices and appreciate each moment of our recovery.

LIVING INTENTIONALLY

Mindful Engagement: Give your full attention to each task, even if they are mundane routine chores.

Align with Your Purpose: Ensure your actions reflect your values and contribute to your goals.

Express Gratitude: Acknowledge the opportunity each moment provides to make a positive impact.

I live each moment fully and intentionally. My actions reflect the best of me.

DAY 218

"Courage doesn't always roar. Sometimes courage is the quiet voice at the end of the day saying, 'I will try again tomorrow.'" MARY ANNE RADMACHER

Persistence in the face of difficulty is a form of courage. Acknowledging our efforts and continuing despite setbacks strengthens our resolve. In recovery, this perseverance is vital for long-term success.

BUILDING GRIT

Acknowledge your Efforts: Recognize and appreciate the small steps you take each day toward your goals.

Learn from Setbacks: View obstacles as learning opportunities rather than failures.

Renew Commitment: At the end of the day, affirm your dedication to continue your journey tomorrow.

I persevere with quiet courage. Each day is a new opportunity for growth.

DAY 219

"He who is brave is free." SENECA

Courage liberates us from the chains of fear and doubt. By facing challenges boldly, we expand our possibilities. In recovery, embracing challenges bravely empowers us to overcome them and welcome new experiences.

EMBRACING BRAVERY

Identify Fears: Acknowledge fears that may be holding you back.

Take a Bold Step: Choose one fear to confront today, even if it is something minor.

Reflect on Freedom Gained: Notice how facing your fear affects your sense of freedom and confidence.

I embrace courage and step beyond my fears. Bravery brings me freedom.

DAY 220

"Each man is questioned by life; and he can only answer to life by answering for his own life; to life he can only respond by being responsible."
VICTOR FRANKL

Our greatest responsibility is to ourselves. While we may have authoritative figures in our lives and people we seek validation from, our first duty is to think and act in accordance with what brings us health and happiness. In recovery, responsibility to ourselves recenters us.

HOLDING OURSELVES RESPONSIBLE

Examine External Sources of Validation: Reflect on the people around you. Do you wish to seek their approval or validation? Observe how this manifests in your actions.

Self-Reflection: Reflect on how the wish to please others affect your thinking and actions. Are your actions balanced or do you find yourself going out of your way? Does it take focus away from yourself and your needs?

Set Personal Standards: Consider what might be a healthy balance. Caring for others shouldn't come at the cost of caring for yourself.

I am responsible for my life, my happiness and my health. I love to care for others, and my care for others comes after care for myself.

DAY 221

"Character is destiny." HERACLITUS

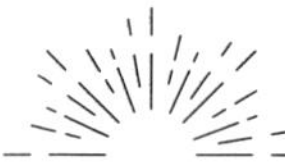

Our characters—the sum of our habits, choices and values—shape the course of our lives. By cultivating virtues like integrity, we steer our destiny toward fulfillment and purpose. In recovery, focusing on character development reinforces our commitment to lasting change.

BUILDING A VIRTUOUS CHARACTER

Identify Core Virtues: Choose virtues you wish to embody, such as honesty, courage or patience.

Daily Actions: Implement specific actions each day that reflect these virtues in your interactions and decisions.

Reflect and Adjust: At the end of the day, assess how well you demonstrated these virtues and consider how you can improve tomorrow.

I choose my action, and my actions determine my character. I choose a virtuous life for myself through happy and healthy choices.

DAY 222

"The only wealth which you will keep forever is the wealth you have given away." MARCUS AURELIUS

Generosity enriches both the giver and the receiver. Sharing our time, resources or kindness creates lasting value beyond material possessions. In recovery, practicing generosity strengthens our connections and brings deeper fulfillment.

EMBRACING GENEROSITY

Give to Others: Identify ways you can offer support or kindness to others today, whether through volunteering, offering to listen to them or other small acts of service.

Practice Selfless Giving: Offer help without expecting anything in return, focusing only on the joy of giving.

Reflect on Impact: Notice how your generosity affects others and enhances your own sense of purpose.

I enrich my life through generosity. Giving brings me lasting fulfillment and joy.

DAY 223

"Suffering becomes beautiful when anyone bears great calamities with cheerfulness, not through insensibility but through greatness of mind." ARISTOTLE

Facing adversity with a positive spirit demonstrates inner strength and resilience. It's not about ignoring pain but about rising above it. In recovery, adopting a courageous attitude toward challenges empowers us to overcome them.

CULTIVATING RESILIENCE

Acknowledge Your Challenges: Recognize difficulties you're experiencing without judgment or self-pity.

Choose a Positive Attitude: Decide to approach these challenges with optimism and determination.

Seek Meaning: Reflect on how overcoming these obstacles contributes to your growth and strengthens your character.

I face adversity with courage and grace. My resilience transforms challenges into growth.

DAY 224

"Be like the cliff against which the waves continually break; but it stands firm and tames the fury of the water around it." MARCUS AURELIUS

Life's storms may rage around us, but by grounding ourselves in our values and inner strength, we can withstand external pressures and remain steadfast and unshaken. In recovery, this stability is crucial for maintaining progress and peace.

ESTABLISHING INNER STRENGTH

Identify Your Foundation: Reflect on the principles and beliefs that anchor you.

Strengthen Your Core: Engage in practices that reinforce your inner stability, such as meditation, journaling or spiritual study.

Stand Firm in Challenges: When faced with difficulties, remind yourself of your foundation and choose responses that reflect your strength.

I am steadfast like a rock. My inner strength carries me through life's storms.

DAY 225

"Curb your desire—don't set your heart on so many things and you will get what you need." EPICTETUS

Continual dissatisfaction prevents us from enjoying what we have. Recognizing when we have enough allows us to experience contentment and peace. In recovery, appreciating sufficiency helps us avoid unhealthy desires and find satisfaction in the present.

PRACTICING SUFFICIENCY

Assess Your Needs vs. Wants: Distinguish between what you truly need and what are unnecessary desires.

Embrace Contentment: Make a conscious decision to appreciate and be satisfied with what you already have.

Avoid Excess: Refrain from pursuing "more" when "enough" meets your needs, focusing instead on non-material fulfillment.

I find contentment in sufficiency. Appreciating what I have brings me peace.

DAY 226

"To be even-minded is the greatest virtue."
HERACLITUS

Maintaining emotional balance allows us to navigate life's ups and downs with grace. By cultivating equanimity, we prevent external events from disrupting our inner peace. In recovery, this steadiness supports sustained well-being.

CULTIVATING EQUANIMITY

Practice Mindfulness: Regularly check in with your emotional state without judgment.

Respond, Don't React: When emotions arise, take a moment to pause and choose a measured response.

Maintain Perspective: Remind yourself that most situations are temporary and can be managed calmly.

I maintain balance and calm. Equanimity guides me through life's fluctuations.

DAY 227

"No man was ever wise by chance." SENECA

Wisdom results from deliberate effort, reflection and learning from experiences. It doesn't happen accidentally. In recovery, seeking knowledge and understanding enhances our journey and helps us make better choices.

PURSUING WISDOM

Engage in Learning: Dedicate time to read, study or engage in discussions that expand your understanding.

Reflect on Experiences: Consider past events and what they have taught you.

Apply Insights: Use the knowledge you've gained to inform your decisions and actions.

I seek wisdom intentionally. My commitment to learning enriches my life.

DAY 228

"If you want to improve, be content to be thought foolish and stupid." EPICTETUS

Fear of judgment can hinder growth, but embracing humility and being open to making mistakes paves the way for improvement. In recovery, acknowledging that we don't have all the answers allows us to learn and evolve.

EMBRACING HUMILITY

Admit Limitations: Acknowledge areas where you have room to grow without self-criticism.

Seek Guidance: Be open to advice and feedback from others, even if it challenges your ego.

Celebrate Learning: View mistakes as opportunities for growth rather than failures.

I embrace humility. Openness to learning strengthens me.

DAY 229

"Time is a created thing. To say, 'I don't have time,' is to say, 'I don't want to.'" LAO TZU

We prioritize what matters to us. Acknowledging this empowers us to take responsibility for how we spend our time. Consciously choosing our activities supports our goals and values in recovery.

PRIORITIZING WISELY

Evaluate Your Time Usage: Track how you spend your time during the day.

Align Actions with Values: Identify tasks that align with your goals and those that don't.

Make Conscious Choices: Adjust your schedule to prioritize meaningful activities.

I choose how I spend my time. My priorities reflect my values and goals.

DAY 230

"Fire tries gold, misfortune tries brave men." SENECA

Challenges refine us, shaping our character and abilities. Embracing trials as part of our growth journey transforms adversities into opportunities. Each trial we overcome strengthens our resolve in our recovery.

EMBRACING GROWTH THROUGH TRIALS

Acknowledge Difficulties: Accept that hardships are natural and necessary for development.

Find the Lesson: Reflect on what each challenge is teaching you.

Express Gratitude: Cultivate appreciation for the growth that comes from overcoming obstacles.

Trials refine me. I grow stronger and wiser through life's challenges.

DAY 231

"Act as if what you do makes a difference. It does."
WILLIAM JAMES

Every action we take contributes to our growth and impacts those around us. Recognizing the significance of our choices empowers us to live intentionally. In recovery, understanding that our efforts matter reinforces our commitment to positive change.

KNOWING YOUR IMPACT

Acknowledge Small Actions: Reflect on daily actions that contribute to your well-being and others'.

Set Intentional Goals: Choose activities today that align with your values and make a positive impact.

Express Gratitude: Thank someone who has positively influenced your life, acknowledging their impact.

My actions make a difference. I choose to contribute positively to the world.

DAY 232

"Well begun is half done." ARISTOTLE

Starting strong sets the tone for the journey ahead. By taking the first step with determination and clarity, we pave the way for success. In recovery, initiating positive habits builds momentum toward a lasting change.

STARTING STRONG

Begin with Purpose: Set clear intentions at the start of your day.

Tackle Important Tasks: Focus on meaningful activities first, when your energy is at its highest.

Maintain Momentum: Celebrate small achievements to keep motivation high.

I begin each day with purpose.
My focused start leads to success.

DAY 233

"No wind favors he who has no destined port."
MICHEL DE MONTAIGNE

Without clear goals, external circumstances cannot guide us. Defining our destination allows us to navigate effectively. In recovery, setting specific objectives directs our efforts and measures progress.

DEFINING YOUR GOALS

Clarify Your Vision: Write down what you aim to achieve in your recovery journey.

Set Measurable Goals: Break down your vision into specific, attainable steps.

Review Regularly: Monitor your progress and adjust your plan as needed.

I chart my course with clear goals. My direction guides my journey.

DAY 234

"Wisdom begins in wonder." SOCRATES

Curiosity opens the door to learning and growth. By approaching life with wonder, we remain open to new insights and experiences. In recovery, this mindset enriches our journey and deepens understanding.

CULTIVATING CURIOSITY

Ask Questions: Seek to understand more about yourself and the world.

Explore New Perspectives: Engage with ideas or activities outside your usual routine.

Embrace Learning Opportunities: View each day as a chance to gain wisdom.

I embrace curiosity. Wonder leads me to wisdom and growth.

DAY 235

"Action is the antidote to despair." JOAN BAEZ

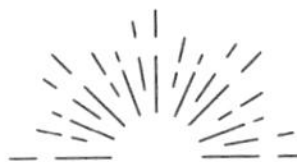

By engaging in purposeful action, we empower ourselves to overcome challenges. Taking proactive steps also combats feelings of hopelessness. Active participation in our healing fosters resilience and optimism in our recovery journey.

TAKING PROACTIVE STEPS

Identify Areas of Inaction: Recognize where inertia may be holding you back.

Choose One Action: Select a meaningful task to tackle today.

Reflect on Progress: Acknowledge how taking action improves your mood and outlook.

I combat despair with action. My steps forward build hope.

DAY 236

"Patience is bitter, but its fruit is sweet." ARISTOTLE

Holding on to patience may be challenging, but it leads to rewarding outcomes. Waiting with grace allows processes to unfold naturally. In recovery, patience supports healing and the development of permanent change.

PRACTICING PATIENCE

Identify Impatience Triggers: Notice situations where you feel rushed or frustrated.

Practice Mindful Breathing: Use deep breaths to center yourself when impatience arises.

Trust the Process: Remind yourself that growth takes time.

I practice patience. I trust that time nurtures growth and brings rewards.

DAY 237

"We become what we think about."
EARL NIGHTINGALE

Our dominant thoughts shape our reality. Focusing on positive, empowering ideas guides us toward our desired outcomes. In recovery, cultivating constructive thoughts fosters transformation.

SHAPING A POSITIVE MINDSET

Monitor Your Thinking: Be aware of recurring thoughts throughout the day.

Choose Positive Focus: Deliberately replace negative thoughts with uplifting ones.

Visualize Success: Imagine yourself achieving your goals and embodying your best self.

My thoughts shape my reality. I think positively to become my best self.

DAY 238

"He who dares not offend cannot be honest."
THOMAS PAINE

Honesty sometimes requires courage to speak uncomfortable truths. Authentic communication fosters trust and integrity. In recovery, embracing honesty strengthens our relationships and self-respect.

PRACTICING HONESTY

Reflect on Truthfulness: Consider areas where you withhold honesty to avoid discomfort.

Communicate Openly: Engage in a sincere conversation where you express your true feelings respectfully.

Accept Reactions: Understand that others may need time to process honesty, and that's acceptable.

I embrace honesty with courage. Truth strengthens my integrity and connections.

DAY 239

"The only limit to our realization of tomorrow will be our doubts of today." FRANKLIN D. ROOSEVELT

Doubt can hinder our progress and potential, but believing in ourselves unlocks possibilities for the future. In recovery, overcoming self-doubt propels us toward our aspirations.

OVERCOMING DOUBTS

Identify Doubts: Reflect on and acknowledge any self-limiting beliefs you hold.

Challenge Negative Beliefs: Question the validity of these doubts and consider evidences to the contrary.

Affirm Your Capabilities: Remind yourself of past successes and strengths

I release doubts. Confidence in myself opens doors to my future.

DAY 240

"Joy is not in things; it is in us." RICHARD WAGNER

With today's quote, Richard Wagner reminds us that true happiness comes from within, not from external possessions. Nurturing the inner joy enhances our experience of life, as focusing on internal fulfillment supports lasting contentment in our recovery journey.

NURTURING INNER JOY

Engage in Self-Care: Participate in activities that bring you genuine happiness.

Practice Mindfulness: Be present and savor the simple moments of joy throughout your day.

Share Positivity: Spread the joy to others through acts of kindness.

Joy resides within me. I cultivate happiness from the inside out.

DAY 241

"We cannot direct the wind, but we can adjust the sails." DOLLY PARTON

Life often presents us with circumstances beyond our control. While we cannot dictate every event, we have the power to choose our responses. In recovery, adapting to challenges, rather than resisting them, allows us to navigate our journey with resilience and grace.

ADAPTING TO CHANGE

Identify Uncontrollable Factors: List aspects of your life that you cannot change. Acknowledge them without frustration.

Focus on Adaptation: Determine how you can adjust your attitude or behavior to better cope with these factors.

Implement Positive Changes: Take actionable steps today to adapt in a way that promotes your well-being.

I adjust my sails to life's winds. By adapting, I steer my journey toward peace and fulfillment.

DAY 242

"The secret of happiness is not found in seeking more but in developing the capacity to enjoy less."
SOCRATES

True contentment comes not from acquiring more but from appreciating what we already have. In recovery, simplifying our desires and embracing gratitude leads to deeper satisfaction and peace.

EMBRACING SIMPLICITY

Declutter Your Space: Choose an area to organize and remove items that no longer serve you.

Mindful Consumption: Before making a purchase, ask yourself if it aligns with your needs or simply fills a temporary desire.

Practice Gratitude: Write down three simple things that bring you joy each day.

I find joy in simplicity. Appreciating minimalism brings me more happiness.

DAY 243

"Happiness is not something ready-made. It comes from your own actions." DALAI LAMA

We are the architects of our own happiness. By engaging in activities and thoughts that align with our values, we cultivate joy from within. With the above quote, the Dalai Lama reminds us that proactive efforts toward our well-being enhances our sense of fulfillment in recovery.

CREATING YOUR HAPPINESS

Engage in a Joyful Activity: Dedicate time to something today that makes you happy.

Perform an Act of Kindness: Help someone in need in whatever way possible, as it can boost your own sense of happiness and purpose.

Reflect on Positive Actions: At the end of the day, note how your actions contributed to your overall happiness.

I create my own happiness through my actions. Joy is a product of my choices.

DAY 244

"The mind is everything. What you think, you become."
THE BUDDHA

Our thoughts shape our reality. By nurturing positive and empowering thoughts, we influence our emotions and actions in constructive ways. In recovery, cultivating a healthy mindset is essential for a lasting transformation.

CULTIVATING POSITIVE THOUGHTS

Monitor Inner Dialogue: Pay attention to negative self-talk and challenge unhelpful thoughts.

Affirm Your Strengths: Write down affirmations that reinforce your self-worth and repeat them throughout the day.

Visualize Success: Spend some time imagining yourself achieving your goals and living in alignment with your values.

My thoughts shape my reality. I choose to think positively and empower myself.

DAY 245

"Peace begins with a smile." MOTHER TERESA

Simple acts like smiling can transform our mood and the atmosphere around us. Embracing positivity fosters inner peace and strengthens our connections with others. In recovery, small gestures, like a kind smile, contribute significantly to our overall well-being.

SPREADING POSITIVITY

Smile Intentionally: Make a conscious effort to smile at people you encounter today.

Offer Kind Words: Compliment someone sincerely or express appreciation.

Reflect on Impact: Notice how these small acts affect your mood and the responses of others.

I cultivate peace through simple acts. My smile brings joy to myself and others.

DAY 246

"You must be the change you wish to see in the world."
MAHATMA GANDHI

Personal transformation inspires change around us. By embodying the qualities we value, we influence our environment positively. Leading by example reinforces our commitment to our recovery journey, as well as influences others around us to embody positive attributes.

BEING THE CHANGE

Identify Desired Changes: Reflect on what you wish to see in the world, like kindness, honesty, compassion.

Embody These Qualities: Choose actions today that reflect these values in your interactions.

Encourage Others: Share your experiences and inspire those around you to join in the positive changes.

I am the change I wish to see. My actions influence the world positively.

DAY 247

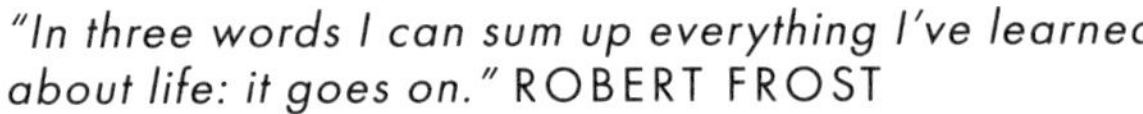

"In three words I can sum up everything I've learned about life: it goes on." ROBERT FROST

Life continues through ups and downs. Accepting this impermanence helps us navigate challenges with resilience in our recovery. Moreover, understanding that difficult moments are temporary encourages perseverance in our journey.

ACCEPTING CHANGE

Accept Change: Acknowledge that change is a natural part of life and growth.

Let Go of Attachment: Practice releasing your expectations of attaining a certain kind of result or your attachments to any specific outcome.

Focus on the Present: Engage fully with the current moment, appreciating its transient beauty.

I embrace life's flow. Change is constant, and I adapt to it with grace.

DAY 248

"Success is not the key to happiness. Happiness is the key to success." ALBERT SCHWEITZER

Pursuing happiness through external achievements often leaves us unfulfilled, while finding joy within ourselves paves the way for true success. Today's quote reminds us that in recovery, prioritizing inner contentment leads to more meaningful accomplishments.

PRIORITIZING INNER JOY

Identify Sources of Joy: Make a list of activities and experiences that bring you genuine happiness.

Schedule Joyful Activities: Dedicate time to engage in these activities regularly.

Redefine Success: Reflect on what success means to you beyond material or external achievements.

Happiness is my foundation. From inner joy, I achieve true success.

DAY 249

"How often has the unexpected happened! How often has the expected never come to pass! ... You will suffer soon enough, when it arrives; so look forward meanwhile to better things." SENECA

Fear of suffering often causes more distress than the event itself. By releasing fear, we alleviate unnecessary pain. Facing fears diminishes their power over us and fosters freedom in our recovery journey.

OVERCOMING FEAR

Identify Your Fears: Write down what you are afraid of and how these fears affect you.

Challenge Fearful Thoughts: Question the likelihood of these events coming to pass and counter your fears with logic.

Take Empowered Action: Choose one of these fears and take one small step today to confront it. Create action plans, such as gradually exposing yourself to the source of your fear.

I release fear and embrace courage. Letting go of fear frees me from unnecessary suffering.

DAY 250

"The greatest glory in living lies not in never falling, but in rising every time we fall." NELSON MANDELA

Setbacks are inevitable, but resilience is found in our ability to rise again. Each time we recover from a fall, we strengthen our character. In recovery, perseverance through difficulties leads to lasting growth.

BUILDING RESILIENCE

Reflect on Past Recoveries: Recall times when you've overcome challenges and how you managed to do so.

Develop Coping Strategies: Identify tools and support systems that help you bounce back.

Embrace the Lesson: View setbacks as opportunities to learn and improve.

I rise stronger each time I fall. My resilience leads me to greatness.

DAY 251

"How does it help...to make troubles heavier by bemoaning them?" SENECA

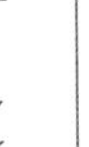

Worrying about the future can lead to fear, stress and anxiety. By projecting fears on to events that haven't occurred, we rob ourselves of present peace. In recovery, focusing on the present moment helps us conserve energy for actual challenges rather than imagined ones.

LETTING GO OF WORRY

Practice Mindfulness: Engage in activities that anchor you to the present moment, such as deep breathing, meditation or yoga.

Challenge Anxious Thoughts: When worries arise, question their validity—whether they are based on facts or assumptions.

Create a Plan: For concerns that require action, outline practical steps you can take, and then release the rest.

I release unnecessary worries and embrace the present. I trust in my ability to handle future challenges as they come.

DAY 252

"To live a good life: We have the potential for it. If we learn to be indifferent to what makes no difference."
MARCUS AURELIUS

Much of our distress comes from attaching importance to things that do not truly matter. By focusing on what is within our control and letting go of trivial concerns, we free ourselves to live more fully. In recovery, this shift in focus enhances our clarity and peace.

RANKING WHAT MATTERS

Identify Core Values: Reflect on what is truly important to you and aligns with your recovery.

Let Go of Trivial Matters: Consciously release thoughts and worries about insignificant issues.

Focus Your Energy: Invest time and effort into activities and relationships that support your well-being and growth.

I focus on what truly matters. Letting go of the trivial brings me clarity and peace.

DAY 253

"The greater the difficulty, the more glory in surmounting it. Skillful pilots gain their reputation from storms and tempests." EPICTETUS

Challenges test our abilities but strengthen our character. Overcoming significant obstacles enhances our confidence and sense of achievement. In recovery, each difficulty faced and surmounted is a testament to our resilience.

EMBRACING CHALLENGES

Face Difficulties Head-On: Identify a challenge you've been avoiding and take the first step toward addressing it.

Seek Support: Reach out to friends, mentors or support groups for assistance and encouragement.

Celebrate Progress: Acknowledge your efforts and growth as you navigate the obstacles.

I meet challenges with courage. Overcoming them strengthens me and brings fulfillment.

DAY 254

"We should always be asking ourselves: 'Is this something that is, or is not, in my control?'" EPICTETUS

Today's quote teaches us that recognizing the difference between what we can and cannot control allows us to direct our energy wisely. This discernment reduces frustration and empowers us to focus on making positive changes where we can in our recovery.

FOCUSING ON WHAT YOU CAN CONTROL

List Your Concerns: Write down every distressing thought currently on your mind.

Categorize Them: Separate the list into things you can control and things you cannot.

Take Action: Devote your efforts to the items that are within your control and practice acceptance for the rest.

I focus on what I can control and accept what I cannot. This brings me peace and empowerment.

DAY 255

"If you want to conquer the anxiety of life, live in the moment, live in the breath." AMIT RAY

Anxiety often stems from ruminating on the past or worrying about the future. Grounding ourselves in the present moment brings relief and clarity. In recovery, mindfulness enhances our ability to cope with stress and enjoy life more fully.

PRACTICING MINDFULNESS

Mindful Breathing: Spend five minutes focusing solely on your breath, feeling each inhale and exhale.

Engage Your Senses: Throughout the day, take moments to notice what you can see, hear, smell, taste and touch.

Mindful Activities: Perform routine tasks with full attention, such as eating slowly and savoring each bite.

I find peace in the present moment. Living mindfully brings me serenity and joy.

DAY 256

"Another person will not hurt you without your cooperation. You are hurt the moment you believe yourself to be." EPICTETUS

We can choose integrity and compassion over hurt and suffering as a result of another's action. In doing so, we free ourselves from the cycle of negativity. This approach promotes healing and inner peace in our recovery.

LETTING GO OF GRUDGES

Identify Resentments: Acknowledge any lingering anger or desire for revenge you may hold.

Practice Forgiveness: Understand that forgiveness is for your benefit, releasing you from the burden of bitterness.

Choose Positive Actions: Respond to negativity with either kindness or disengagement, maintaining your own standards.

I release resentment and choose compassion. I am not harmed if I choose not to be.

DAY 257

"Imagine for yourself a character, a model personality, whose example you determine to follow, in private as well as in public." EPICTETUS

Today's quote reminds us that clarity about our desired identity guides our actions toward becoming that person. Setting a vision for ourselves provides direction and motivation. This self-definition is a powerful tool for transformation in our recovery.

DEFINING YOUR IDEAL SELF

Visualize Your Best Self: Like the quote suggests, imagine in detail the person you want to be in terms of character, habits and impact.

Set Specific Goals: Identify the steps needed to embody these qualities.

Take Daily Actions: Adopt habits and behaviors that align with your vision.

I am becoming the person I aspire to be. My actions today reflect my highest self.

DAY 258

"All of our life is but a mass of small habits—practical, emotional, intellectual and spiritual—that bear us irresistibly toward our destiny." WILLIAM JAMES

Consistency in our actions shapes our character and destiny, and by establishing positive habits, we lay the foundation for excellence. In recovery, daily practices reinforce our commitment and further our progress.

BUILDING POSITIVE HABITS

Identify Key Habits: Choose one habit that will significantly impact your well-being.

Create a Plan: Outline how you will integrate this habit into your daily routine.

Monitor Progress: Keep a log of your adherence and reflect on the benefits you experience

My habits define me. I cultivate practices that lead to excellence and fulfillment.

DAY 259

"He who knows that enough is enough will always have enough." LAO TZU

Contentment arises from appreciating sufficiency rather than seeking excess. So, recognizing when we have enough brings peace and satisfaction. In recovery, this mindset helps us avoid cravings and find joy in simplicity.

PRACTICING CONTENTMENT

Gratitude Inventory: List the things you have that meet your needs and bring you happiness.

Avoid Comparison: Refrain from measuring your life against others'; focus on your own path.

Mindful Consumption: Before acquiring more, consider whether it adds genuine value to your life.

I have enough, and I am enough. Contentment fills my heart and life.

DAY 260

"Do not go where the path may lead, go instead where there is no path and leave a trail."
RALPH WALDO EMERSON

Following our own unique journey allows us to live authentically and make meaningful contributions. Forging our own path fosters self-discovery and fulfillment in our recovery journey as well.

EMBRACING YOUR UNIQUE JOURNEY

Reflect on Your Passions: Identify what truly inspires and motivates you.

Take Initiative: Begin a project or pursue an interest that aligns with your authentic self.

Share Your Journey: Encourage others by sharing your experiences and the lessons you've learned.

I create my own path with courage and authenticity. My journey inspires others and fulfills me.

DAY 261

"The obstacle is the path." ZEN PROVERB

Challenges are not just roadblocks but integral parts of our journey. By embracing obstacles, we transform them into opportunities for growth. Moreover, viewing difficulties as essential steps helps us stay motivated and resilient in our recovery.

EMBRACING OBSTACLES

Identify Current Challenges: List the obstacles you're facing in your recovery journey.

Find the Lesson: Reflect on what each obstacle is teaching you about yourself.

Take Constructive Action: Develop a plan to address these challenges positively.

I embrace obstacles as opportunities. Each challenge strengthens me and guides my growth.

DAY 262

"To bear trials with a calm mind robs misfortune of its strength and burden." SENECA

Our thoughts shape our experiences, and it is in our power to ground our thoughts and keep a peaceful outlook through tough times. Moments in our life may be challenging but it is not until we lose control of our comportment, with rash or impulsive actions, that the distress we feel is amplified. In recovery, learning to maintain our peace can ensure difficult times become manageable situations.

SHIFTING PERSPECTIVES AND MAINTAINING PEACE

Recall a Recent Setback: Think of an unpleasant event and how it made you feel. Then think about how you finally calmed down.

Analyze Your Perception: Consider how you processed the situation and how you acted based on your thoughts and feelings.

Prepare for the Next Challenge: Reflect on your past behaviors and identify ways that help you keep your calm.

I can stay anchored through turbulence. I see challenges as opportunities to recenter my sense of serenity with the world.

DAY 263

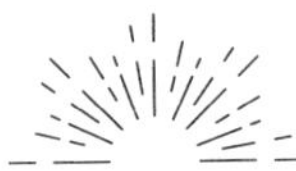

"If it is not right, do not do it; if it is not true, do not say it." MARCUS AURELIUS

Integrity involves aligning our actions and words with our values. This consistency builds trust and self-respect. In recovery, living with integrity supports our healing and strengthens our relationships.

LIVING WITH INTEGRITY

Assess Your Actions: Reflect on whether your recent actions align with your values.

Speak Truthfully: Commit to honesty in your communications today.

Align Intentions and Actions: Ensure that what you intend matches what you do.

I act and speak with integrity. My values guide my choices.

DAY 264

"You have power over your mind—not outside events. Realize this, and you will find strength."
MARCUS AURELIUS

Focusing on controlling our thoughts and reactions empowers us, while accepting that we cannot control external events reduces frustration. In recovery, this internal focus fosters resilience and peace.

CULTIVATING STRENGTH

Monitor Your Thoughts: Pay attention to your internal dialogue throughout the day.

Practice Mindfulness: When stressed, bring your focus back to your breath and the present moment.

Choose Your Reactions: Before responding to external events, pause and decide how you want to react.

I control my thoughts and reactions. My strength comes from within.

DAY 265

"Do not seek to have events happen as you want them to, but instead want them to happen as they do happen, and all will be well with you." EPICTETUS

With today's quote, Epictetus reminds us that accepting reality as it is, rather than how we wish it to be, brings peace. Resisting what we cannot change leads to unnecessary suffering. Hence, embracing acceptance helps us focus on growth in our recovery journey.

PRACTICING ACCEPTANCE

Acknowledge Reality: Identify situations you're resisting and accept them as they are.

Let Go of Control: Recognize what is beyond your influence and release the need to control it.

Focus on Response: Direct your energy toward how you can positively respond to circumstances.

I accept life as it is. Embracing reality brings me peace.

DAY 266

"Happiness is a good flow of life." ZENO OF CITIUM

True happiness comes from living in harmony with our values and the natural flow of life. When we align our actions with our principles, we experience contentment. This alignment is a key to sustained well-being in recovery.

ALIGNING ACTIONS WITH YOUR VALUES

Identify Your Core Values: Write down the principles that are most important to you.

Evaluate Your Actions: Reflect on how your daily activities align with these values.

Make Adjustments: Plan the changes needed to better align your actions with your core beliefs.

I live in harmony with my values. This alignment brings me true happiness.

DAY 267

"No man is free who is not master of himself."
EPICTETUS

Today's quote reminds us that self-mastery is essential for true freedom. It involves controlling our impulses and emotions rather than being controlled by them. In recovery, developing this self-discipline empowers us to make healthy choices.

ENHANCING SELF-CONTROL

Identify Triggers: Note situations where you feel as if you are losing control.

Develop Strategies: Create plans to manage these triggers with healthy coping mechanisms like journaling or taking alternative actions.

Practice Discipline: Set small goals to strengthen your self-control, like sticking to a routine.

I am the master of my actions and emotions. Self-control brings me freedom.

DAY 268

"He is a wise man who does not grieve for the things which he has not but rejoices for those which he has."
EPICTETUS

Gratitude shifts our focus from lack to abundance. Appreciating what we have fosters contentment and joy. In recovery as well, practicing gratitude strengthens our resilience and optimism.

CULTIVATING GRATITUDE

Gratitude Journaling: Write down five things you're grateful for today.

Express Thanks: Share your appreciation with someone who has positively impacted your life.

Mindful Appreciation: Throughout the day, consciously acknowledge moments of goodness.

My heart is filled with gratitude.
I cherish the abundance in my life.

DAY 269

"Be tolerant with others and strict with yourself."
MARCUS AURELIUS

Holding ourselves accountable while showing compassion to others fosters personal growth and harmonious relationships. In recovery, this approach helps us improve without becoming judgmental.

BALANCING COMPASSION AND ACCOUNTABILITY

Self-Improvement Plan: Identify areas where you can grow and set specific goals.

Practice Empathy: When others err, respond with understanding rather than criticism.

Lead by Example: Demonstrate your values through your actions, inspiring others.

I strive for excellence within and show compassion to others. This balance enriches my life.

DAY 270

"When you arise in the morning, think of what a precious privilege it is to be alive—to breathe, to think, to enjoy, to love." MARCUS AURELIUS

Happiness is found in embracing the present moment rather than fixating on future outcomes. Letting go of anxiety about what may come allows us to experience joy now. Focusing on the present moment supports serenity and fulfillment in our recovery journey.

EMBRACING THE PRESENT

Mindful Activities: Engage in tasks today with full attention, savoring each experience.

Release Future Worries: When anxious thoughts arise, gently bring your focus back to the present.

Create Moments of Joy: Do something today simply for the pleasure it brings you now.

I live fully in the present moment. Embracing the now brings me true happiness.

DAY 271

"Be content with what you have; rejoice in the way things are. When you realize there is nothing lacking, the whole world belongs to you." LAO TZU

Contentment arises from appreciating what we have rather than longing for what we don't. In recovery, embracing gratitude for the present moment strengthens our resilience and joy.

PURSUING CONTENTMENT

Appreciate the Present: Spend time today acknowledging the blessings in your life.

Avoid Comparisons: Refrain from comparing yourself to others; focus on your unique journey.

Practice Gratitude: Write down three things you're thankful for at the end of the day.

I have enough in this moment. By accepting what is, I rest in contentment and clarity.

DAY 272

"He who conquers others is strong; he who conquers himself is mighty." LAO TZU

True strength comes from self-mastery. By overcoming our inner challenges and controlling our impulses, we achieve personal freedom. In recovery too, self-discipline empowers us to make choices that align with our highest good.

DEVELOPING SELF-MASTERY

Identify Internal Struggles: Acknowledge areas where you struggle with self-control.

Set Clear Intentions: Define specific goals to overcome these challenges.

Practice Mindfulness: Use techniques like meditation to enhance self-awareness and control.

I am the master of my thoughts and actions. Through self-discipline, I achieve true strength.

DAY 273

"The only true wisdom is in knowing you know nothing."
SOCRATES

Embracing humility opens us to continuous learning. Recognizing that there's always more to understand keeps us curious and receptive. This mindset allows us to grow and adapt more effectively in our recovery journey.

EMBRACING LIFELONG LEARNING

Adopt a Beginner's Mind: Think of each day as an opportunity to learn something new.

Seek Knowledge: Read a book, attend a workshop or engage in meaningful conversations.

Reflect on Lessons Learned: At the end of the day, note what you've discovered or understood differently.

I embrace humility and the pursuit of wisdom. Each day offers new insights.

DAY 274

"The journey of a thousand miles begins with one step."
LAO TZU

Progress is made through small, consistent actions. Each step, no matter how small, moves us closer to our goals. In recovery, acknowledging and celebrating these steps builds momentum and confidence.

TAKING THE FIRST STEP

Identify a Goal: Choose a goal you've been wanting to achieve.

Break It Down: Divide the goal into manageable steps.

Take Action Today: Begin with the first step today, no matter how small.

I move forward one step at a time. Each action brings me closer to my aspirations.

DAY 275

"It does not matter how slowly you go as long as you do not stop." CONFUCIUS

After taking the first step, persistence is key to achieving our objectives. Progress may be gradual but steady effort leads to significant change over time. In recovery, patience with ourselves supports sustained growth.

EMBRACING PERSISTENCE

Acknowledge Progress: Recognize and appreciate the advancements you've made, regardless of pace.

Stay Committed: Reaffirm your dedication to your goals daily.

Overcome Setbacks: View obstacles as temporary and continue moving forward.

I persist in the face of challenges. My steady efforts lead to success.

DAY 276

"You are today where your thoughts have brought you; you will be tomorrow where your thoughts take you."
JAMES ALLEN

Our thoughts shape our reality. By nurturing positive and constructive thoughts, we influence our actions and experiences. This is why cultivating a healthy mindset is essential for transformation in our recovery journey.

CULTIVATING POSITIVE THOUGHTS

Monitor Inner Dialogue: Be aware of negative self-talk and replace it with affirming statements.

Visualize Success: Spend some time in the day imagining yourself achieving your goals.

Surround Yourself with Positivity: Engage with people and environments that uplift you.

My thoughts create my reality. I choose to think positively and empower myself.

DAY 277

"Whoever values peace of mind and the health of the soul will live the best of all possible lives."
MARCUS AURELIUS

True peace is cultivated internally; it is not found in external circumstances. By nurturing our inner world, we create a foundation of serenity. In recovery, this inner peace supports resilience against external stresses.

NURTURING INNER PEACE

Meditation Practice: Dedicate time to quiet reflection or meditation.

Release External Dependence: Recognize when you're seeking validation or peace from outside sources.

Cultivate Self-Compassion: Treat yourself with kindness and understanding.

Peace resides within me. I nurture my inner tranquility.

DAY 278

"He who is not courageous enough to take risks will accomplish nothing in life." MUHAMMAD ALI

Taking risks is essential for growth and achievement, as stepping out of our comfort zone opens doors to new opportunities. In our recovery journey also, embracing calculated risks can lead to profound personal development.

EMBRACING COURAGE

Identify a Fear: Recognize an area where fear is holding you back.

Take a Small Risk: Commit to an action that challenges this fear.

Reflect on the Outcome: Consider what you've learned from taking this risk.

I face my fears with courage. Taking risks leads me to growth and accomplishment.

DAY 279

"You may encounter many defeats, but you must not be defeated." MAYA ANGELOU

Resilience is demonstrated by our ability to recover from setbacks. Each time we rise after a fall, we strengthen our character. Persevering even after setbacks is the key to long-term success.

BUILDING RESILIENCE

Learn from Setbacks: Reflect on what a recent challenge has taught you.

Develop Coping Strategies: Identify tools that help you bounce back.

Maintain Hope: Keep a positive outlook on your journey ahead.

I rise stronger after every fall. Resilience guides my path to success.

DAY 280

"Never act without purpose and resolve, or without the means to finish the job." MARCUS AURELIUS

A strong sense of purpose helps us endure difficulties and live a meaningful life. Today's quote reminds us that knowing our "why" provides motivation and direction, and in recovery, identifying our reasons for change fuels perseverance.

DISCOVERING YOUR PURPOSE

Reflect on Your Motivations: Write down why recovery is important to you.

Set Meaningful Goals: Align your actions with your deeper purpose.

Remind Yourself Daily: Keep your "why" visible by writing it in your journal to reinforce your commitment.

My purpose is to _______ because _______ , and I will start by _______.

DAY 281

"Act with kindness, but do not expect gratitude."
CONFUCIUS

True kindness is given freely, without expecting anything in return. By acting generously without seeking acknowledgment, we encourage a pure heart and avoid disappointment. In recovery, this selfless approach strengthens our character and deepens our relationships.

PRACTICING SELFLESS KINDNESS

Perform an Anonymous Act: Do something kind for someone without revealing your identity.

Release Expectations: When helping others, focus on the act itself rather than any potential acknowledgment you may or may not receive.

Reflect on Giving: Notice how selfless acts affect your sense of fulfillment.

I give freely without expectation. Kindness nourishes my spirit.

DAY 282

"Wisdom begins in wonder." SOCRATES

Curiosity opens the door to deeper understanding. By approaching life with a sense of wonder, we remain receptive to learning and growth. In recovery, nurturing curiosity helps us discover new insights about ourselves and the world.

CULTIVATING CURIOSITY

Ask Questions: Challenge yourself to learn something new today.

Explore New Ideas: Read or listen to perspectives different from your own.

Embrace Learning Opportunities: Attend a workshop or engage in a meaningful conversation.

I embrace curiosity. Wonder leads me to wisdom.

DAY 283

"Silence is a source of great strength." LAO TZU

In moments of quiet, we find clarity and inner peace. Today's quote reminds us that embracing silence allows us to listen to our inner voice and gain strength. Taking time for stillness supports our emotional well-being in our recovery journey as well.

EMBRACING SILENCE

Schedule Quiet Time: Set aside moments in your day for silent reflection.

Mindful Breathing: Focus on your breath to center yourself.

Listen Within: Pay attention to your thoughts and feelings without judgment.

In silence, I find strength and clarity. Stillness restores me.

DAY 284

"Patience is the companion of wisdom."
ST. AUGUSTINE

By practicing patience, we cultivate wisdom and understanding. It allows us to make thoughtful decisions and avoid impulsive actions. In recovery as well, patience is essential for enduring challenges and embracing growth.

PRACTICING PATIENCE

Pause Before Reacting: Take a moment before responding in conversations.

Embrace Waiting: Use times of delay as opportunities for mindfulness.

Reflect on Growth: Consider how patience has benefited you in the past.

I practice patience because through patience, I gain wisdom.

DAY 285

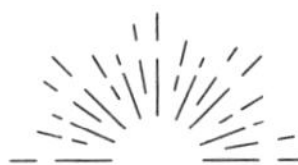

"Loss is nothing else but change, and change is Nature's delight." MARCUS AURELIUS

Change is an inevitable part of life and accepting this truth allows us to adapt and grow. In recovery, embracing change helps us move forward and let go of the past.

EMBRACING CHANGE

Acknowledge Transitions: Recognize areas in your life that are evolving.

Adapt Positively: Find ways to adjust your perspective to accommodate changes.

Let Go of Resistance: Release attachment to how things used to be.

I embrace change. Adaptability strengthens me.

DAY 286

"Knowing yourself is the beginning of all wisdom."
ARISTOTLE

Self-awareness is the foundation of personal growth. By understanding our thoughts, emotions and motivations, we make informed choices. In recovery, knowing ourselves deeply aids in healing and transformation.

GROWING SELF-AWARENESS

Self-Reflection: Spend time journaling about your feelings and behaviors.

Identify Patterns: Notice recurring themes in your thoughts or actions.

Seek Feedback: Consider others' perspectives to gain additional insights.

I know myself deeply. Self-awareness guides my growth.

DAY 287

"Happiness depends upon ourselves." ARISTOTLE

We hold the key to our own happiness. By choosing positive thoughts and actions, we create joy from within. Taking responsibility for our happiness during our recovery journey empowers us.

CREATING YOUR HAPPINESS

Engage in Enjoyable Activities: Do something today that brings you joy.

Positive Affirmations: Remind yourself of your strengths and achievements.

Share Happiness: Spread joy to others through kind gestures.

I create my own happiness. Joy is my choice.

DAY 288

"If you want a quality, act as if you already have it. If you want to be courageous, act as if you were—and as you act and persevere in acting, so you tend to become." NORMAN VINCENT PEALE

Our actions shape our identity, and by embodying the person we aspire to be, we transform ourselves. In recovery as well, intentional actions lead to a lasting change.

EMBODYING YOUR ASPIRATIONS

Define Your Ideal Self: Note down the qualities you wish to embody.

Align Your Actions: Make choices that reflect these qualities.

Consistent Practice: Commit to daily behaviors that reinforce your desired identity.

I have the qualities of the person I want to become. My actions transform me.

DAY 289

"To love oneself is the beginning of a lifelong romance."
OSCAR WILDE

Our primary companion through life is ourselves; therefore, loving ourselves should be at the core of our goals. It's a process, and we start with simple gestures that have profound effects. In recovery, small acts of kindness toward ourselves enhance our well-being.

BEING YOUR OWN COMPANION

Think About Yourself: Imagine meeting yourself at a social event. What would you immediately observe and like about yourself?

Analyze Your Relationship with Yourself: Think about your relationship with yourself as if you were a friend. Reflect on the ups and downs of your relationship—when you have been a good companion and when you have been a bad friend.

Be Your Friend: Pick an activity that you can do regularly "with" yourself—an activity where you engage with yourself like you would do with a friend or a partner.

I am my own best friend, lover and companion, and I will treasure this relationship above all else.

DAY 290

"Well done is better than well said."
BENJAMIN FRANKLIN

With today's quote, Benjamin Franklin reinforces that actions speak louder than words. By demonstrating our values through deeds, we make a meaningful impact. In recovery as well, consistent actions reinforce our commitments.

PRIORITIZING ACTION

Set an Action Plan: Identify tasks that align with your goals.

Take Initiative: Begin working on these tasks without delay.

Evaluate Outcomes: Reflect on how your actions advance your objectives.

I let my actions speak. Through deeds, I honor my commitments.

DAY 291

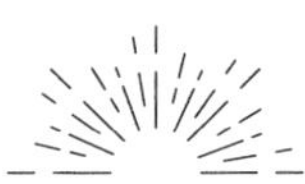

"When force of circumstance upsets your equanimity, lose no time in recovering your self-control, and do not remain out of tune longer than you can help."
MARCUS AURELIUS

We may often lose ourselves in moments of high energy and emotion, but amid these moments, it's essential that our inner world is at peace. By focusing on our inner world—our thoughts, emotions and beliefs—we can make meaningful changes that reflect outwardly. In recovery, nurturing our inner selves is essential for continuous healing and growth.

THE INWARD JOURNEY

Meditate: Spend time in quiet reflection, allowing thoughts to come and go without judgment.

Journaling: Write about your feelings and experiences to gain deeper insight.

Self-Compassion: Practice kindness toward yourself, acknowledging your efforts and progress.

I journey within to discover my true self. My inward journey brings clarity and peace.

DAY 292

"We are shaped by our thoughts; we become what we think." THE BUDDHA

Our minds have powerful influence over our lives. By cultivating positive and constructive thoughts, we shape ourselves into the people we aspire to be. In recovery, focusing on uplifting thoughts supports our healing journey.

MINDFUL THINKING

Thought Awareness: Monitor your thoughts throughout the day, noting any negative patterns.

Positive Affirmations: Replace negative thoughts with positive statements about yourself.

Visualization: Imagine yourself achieving your goals and living in alignment with your values.

My thoughts shape my reality. I choose to think positively and empower myself.

DAY 293

"He who is contented is rich." LAO TZU

True wealth is found in contentment, not in material possessions. By appreciating what we have, we experience a richness that external things cannot provide. In recovery as well, cultivating contentment brings peace and satisfaction.

PRACTICING CONTENTMENT

Gratitude List: Write down things you are grateful for each day.

Mindful Appreciation: Take time to savor simple pleasures—a meal, a conversation, a sunset.

Limit Comparisons: Focus on your own journey without comparing yourself to others.

I am content with what I have. Gratitude fills my life with abundance.

DAY 294

"The unexamined life is not worth living." SOCRATES

Self-reflection is crucial for personal growth, as in examining our lives, we gain insights that lead to better choices and fulfillment. Introspection helps us understand our behaviors and fosters healing in recovery.

PRACTICING REFLECTION

Daily Review: At the end of the day, reflect on your actions and thoughts.

Identify Patterns: Notice recurring themes or behaviors that may need adjustment.

Set Intentions: Use your reflections to set goals for personal improvement.

I examine my life with honesty and openness. Self-reflection leads to growth.

DAY 295

"Happiness is not something ready-made. It comes from your own actions." DALAI LAMA

We create our own happiness through our choices and actions. By engaging in activities that align with our values, we cultivate joy from within. In recovery, proactive efforts toward well-being enhance our fulfillment.

CREATING HAPPINESS

Engage in Joyful Activities: Do something today that brings you genuine joy.

Acts of Kindness: Make someone else's day brighter through a kind gesture.

Reflect on Positive Moments: At the end of the day, recall the moments that made you the happiest.

I create my own happiness through my actions. Joy flows from within me.

DAY 296

"The greatest wealth is to live content with little." PLATO

Simplicity brings freedom and peace. By reducing our attachment to material possessions, we can focus on what truly matters. In our recovery journey too, embracing simplicity helps us find clarity and purpose.

EMBRACING SIMPLICITY

Declutter: Simplify your environment by removing unnecessary items.

Mindful Consumption: Consider your needs versus wants before making purchases.

Value Experiences Over Things: Focus more on creating memories and nurturing relationships.

I find richness in simplicity. Contentment fills my life.

DAY 297

"No man ever steps in the same river twice, for it's not the same river and he's not the same man."
HERACLITUS

Change is constant, and we are always evolving. Embracing this truth allows us to adapt and grow. In recovery, accepting change helps us move forward with resilience.

EMBRACING CHANGE

Acknowledge Growth: Reflect on how you've changed over time.

Stay Open-Minded: Be receptive to new ideas and experiences.

Adapt Flexibly: When faced with change, look for opportunities to grow, rather than resisting.

I embrace change as a natural part of life. Growth comes through adaptation.

DAY 298

"Do not dwell in the past, do not dream of the future; concentrate the mind on the present moment." THE BUDDHA

Today's quote reminds us that living in the present allows us to fully experience life. By releasing past regrets and future anxieties, we find peace and clarity. Similarly, in recovery, mindfulness enhances our ability to enjoy each moment.

BEING PRESENT IN THIS MOMENT

Mindful Breathing: Focus on your breath to anchor yourself in the now.

Engage Fully: Give your full attention to the task or person before you.

Let Go of Distractions: Gently redirect your thoughts to the now when they wander to the past or the future.

I live fully in the present moment. Peace and joy are found here and now.

DAY 299

"The secret of change is to focus all of your energy not on fighting the old but on building the new."
SOCRATES

Progress comes from creating new paths rather than resisting the old ones. By channeling our energy into positive actions, we facilitate transformation. Our focus on building a better future propels us forward in our recovery journey as well.

BUILDING THE NEW

Set Positive Goals: Identify what you want to achieve moving forward.

Take Action: Outline and begin tasks that lead toward your goals.

Release the Past: Acknowledge the past but concentrate more on present efforts.

I focus on building a better future. My energy creates positive change.

DAY 300

"No person has the power to have everything they want, but it is in their power not to want what they don't have." SENECA

Desire, envy and temptation are alluring but chasing them can send us down a path of greed and misery. Counting your blessings and finding contentment with all you are given is the peaceful path, and acceptance will help us find meaning and beauty in the world around and within us in our recovery.

RECOGNISING UNHEALTHY DESIRES

Identify Your Desires: Note the wants that incite negative thoughts and uncharacteristic behaviors.

Determine Their Value: Sit and ponder whether, and if so, then how and why your life will be better once you achieve these desires.

Reflection: Note down what you already have in your life that is beautiful.

I have enough. If my desires evoke hostile and negative thoughts within me, I will not seek those desires.

DAY 301

"He who conquers himself is the mightiest warrior."
CONFUCIUS

Confucius, with today's quote, reminds us that true strength lies not in dominating others but in mastering oneself. By overcoming our own weaknesses and impulses, we achieve a form of victory that external conquests cannot match. This self-discipline and awareness are the keys to a lasting change.

CULTIVATING SELF-MASTERY

Identify Personal Challenges: Reflect on areas where you struggle with self-control or discipline.

Set Specific Goals: Establish clear, achievable objectives to improve in these areas.

Monitor Progress: Keep a daily journal to track your efforts and celebrate small victories.

I am my own greatest warrior. Through self-mastery, I achieve true strength.

DAY 302

"The world will ask you who you are, and if you don't know, the world will tell you." CARL JUNG

Self-knowledge is the foundation of wisdom. By delving deep into our thoughts, emotions and motivations, we gain insights that help us navigate the world more effectively. In recovery, understanding ourselves enables us to identify triggers and develop healthier coping strategies.

BUILDING SELF-AWARENESS

Self-Examination: Spend some time journaling about your beliefs, fears and desires.

Mindful Observation: Notice your reactions in different situations without judgment.

Seek Feedback: Discuss your observations with a trusted friend or mentor for additional perspectives.

I seek to understand myself. Self-awareness guides my journey toward wisdom.

DAY 303

"Change your thoughts and you change your world."
NORMAN VINCENT PEALE

Our thoughts have a profound impact on our reality. By cultivating positive and constructive thinking patterns, we shape ourselves into the people we aspire to be. In recovery, focusing on empowering thoughts aids in overcoming challenges and fostering growth.

SHAPING YOUR MINDSET

Affirm Positive Thoughts: Begin your day with affirmations that reinforce your goals.

Challenge Negativity: When negative thoughts arise, question their validity and replace them with positive alternatives.

Visualize Success: Imagine yourself achieving your recovery goals and living a fulfilling life.

My thoughts shape my reality. I choose to think positively and empower myself.

DAY 304

"An untroubled mind, no longer seeking to consider what is right and what is wrong, a mind beyond judgments, watches and understands." THE BUDDHA

Letting go of constant judgments frees us from unnecessary stress and allows us to experience life more fully. In recovery, practicing non-judgment helps us accept ourselves and others, fostering inner peace and healthier relationships.

BEING NON-JUDGMENTAL

Mindful Awareness: Observe your thoughts and feelings without labeling them as good or bad.

Release Criticism: When you notice yourself judging others, pause and redirect your thoughts.

Embrace Acceptance: Accept situations and people as they are, focusing on understanding rather than evaluating them.

I release judgments and embrace understanding. Peace fills my mind as I accept what is.

DAY 305

"Your vision will become clear only when you look into your heart. Who looks outside, dreams; who looks inside, awakens." CARL JUNG

True clarity comes from introspection. By looking within, we awaken to our true selves and purposes. Self-exploration in recovery is essential for healing and discovering what genuinely fulfills us.

ENGAGING IN DEEPER REFLECTIONS

Heart-Centered Meditation: Spend time focusing on your heart, noticing any feelings or insights that arise.

Identify Core Desires: Reflect on what truly matters to you beyond external expectations.

Align Actions with Values: Make decisions that reflect your inner truths and passions.

I look within to find clarity. My heart guides me toward my true path.

DAY 306

"Simplicity is the ultimate sophistication."
LEONARDO DA VINCI

Embracing simplicity brings clarity and peace to our lives. By eliminating unnecessary complexities, we focus on what truly matters. In our recovery journey, simplifying our environment and routines can reduce stress and support our healing process.

EMBRACING SIMPLICITY

Declutter Spaces: Choose an area to organize and remove items that no longer serve you.

Simplify Commitments: Assess your schedule and prioritize activities that align with your values.

Mindful Consumption: Be intentional about what you bring into your life, from possessions to information.

I find sophistication in simplicity. By simplifying my life, I create space for peace and joy.

DAY 307

"He who knows, does not speak. He who speaks, does not know." LAO TZU

Wisdom often comes with humility and quiet confidence. By listening more and speaking less, we open ourselves to learning and understanding. Practicing active listening enhances our relationships and personal growth in recovery.

CULTIVATING LISTENING SKILLS

Practice Silence: Allow others to speak without interrupting, fully engaging with their words.

Reflect Before Responding: Take a moment to consider your words carefully before speaking.

Seek to Understand: Ask open-ended questions to deepen your comprehension of others' perspectives.

I listen more and speak less. Through silence, I gain wisdom and understanding.

DAY 308

"Never let the future disturb you. You will meet it, if you have to, with the same weapons of reason which today arm you against the present." MARCUS AURELIUS

Worrying about future problems amplifies our suffering unnecessarily. By staying present and dealing with challenges as they arise, we conserve our emotional energy. In recovery, focusing on the present moment aids in reducing anxiety and stress.

REDUCING WORRY

Stay Present: Engage in mindfulness exercises to anchor yourself in the current moment.

Challenge Catastrophizing: When worries about the future arise, assess their realism and likelihood.

Develop Coping Plans: For legitimate concerns, create actionable steps to deal with them rather than merely dwelling on them.

I release unnecessary worries. I face challenges as they come with clarity and calm.

DAY 309

"We do not see things as they are, we see them as we are." ANAÏS NIN

Our perceptions are colored by our experiences, beliefs and emotions. Recognizing this helps us approach situations with greater openness and empathy. Challenging our assumptions in recovery can lead to deeper understanding and healing.

EXPANDING PERCEPTIONS

Question Assumptions: Reflect on beliefs that may be limiting your perspective.

Seek Diverse Views: Engage with people who have different experiences and viewpoints.

Practice Empathy: Try to understand situations from others' perspectives.

I open my mind to new perspectives. By seeing beyond myself, I grow in understanding.

DAY 310

"The bravest sight in the world is to see a great man struggling against adversity." SENECA

Adversity, obstacles and setbacks are a natural part of any journey. Seneca, with today's quote, reminds us that what defines us is not the fall but the strength and determination to get back up and face our challenges. In recovery, resilience is the key to overcoming obstacles and continuing progress.

BUILDING RESILIENCE

Reflect on Past Recoveries: Recall times when you've bounced back from difficulties. Note how you found the courage and what actions you took to persist.

Develop a Support System: Identify people and resources that can help you during challenging times.

Maintain a Growth Mindset: View setbacks as opportunities to learn and strengthen yourself.

I rise stronger after every fall. Resilience carries me forward on my journey.

DAY 311

"Strength does not come from physical capacity. It comes from an indomitable will."
MAHATMA GANDHI

True strength is rooted in our determination and resilience, and it's our unwavering will that empowers us to overcome obstacles and persist in the face of challenges. In recovery too, cultivating an indomitable spirit helps us navigate difficulties and stay committed to our path.

CULTIVATING STRENGTH

Set Clear Intentions: Define your purpose and what you are determined to achieve in your recovery journey.

Embrace Challenges: View obstacles as opportunities to strengthen your willpower and resilience.

Practice Self-Motivation: Use affirmations and positive self-talk to reinforce your determination.

My strength comes from within. My unwavering will guides me through all challenges.

DAY 312

"Man is affected not by changing events but by the view he takes of them." EPICTETUS

Our destiny is shaped by our choices and actions. By consciously deciding who we want to be, we take control of our future. In recovery, this control empowers us to create a life aligned with our true selves and aspirations.

SHAPING YOUR DESTINY

Define Your Vision: Clearly articulate the qualities and the life you desire.

Make Conscious Choices: Ensure your daily decisions align with your vision.

Commit to Action: Take consistent steps toward becoming the person you aspire to be.

I choose who I become. My decisions today shape my destiny.

DAY 313

"The more we value things outside our control, the less control we have." EPICTETUS

Today's quote emphasizes that placing too much importance on external factors diminishes our sense of autonomy. By focusing on what we can control—our thoughts and actions—we empower ourselves. In recovery, this perspective helps us maintain balance and inner peace.

FOCUSING ON WHAT YOU CAN CONTROL

Identify Uncontrollable Factors: Acknowledge things outside your influence that may be causing you stress.

Redirect Your Focus: Concentrate on your reactions and choices in response to these factors.

Practice Acceptance: Let go of the need to control the uncontrollable and embrace serenity instead.

I focus on what I can control. Letting go brings me peace and empowerment.

DAY 314

"It is not death that a man should fear, but he should fear never beginning to live." MARCUS AURELIUS

The true tragedy is not in life's end but in failing to fully embrace and experience it. Embracing life wholeheartedly enriches our recovery journey, as well as brings fulfillment.

EMBRACING LIFE FULLY

Engage in New Experiences: Try something you've always wanted to but haven't yet pursued.

Live Mindfully: Be present in each moment, savoring the experiences of daily life.

Express Gratitude: Acknowledge the gift of life by appreciating the small joys it offers.

I choose to live fully and fearlessly. Each moment is an opportunity to embrace life.

DAY 315

"Courage is not the absence of fear but the triumph over it." NELSON MANDELA

Courage involves facing our fears and moving forward despite them. It's through overcoming fear that we grow stronger, and in recovery, embracing courage propels us toward healing and personal growth.

FACING YOUR FEARS

Identify a Fear: Recognize a fear that is holding you back.

Take a Brave Step: Decide on and take one action that confronts this fear directly.

Reflect on the Experience: Afterward, consider how facing your fear has impacted you.

I face my fears with courage. Overcoming them strengthens me.

DAY 316

"The happiness of your life depends upon the quality of your thoughts." MARCUS AURELIUS

Our mindset significantly influences our overall well-being. By nurturing positive and constructive thoughts, we enhance our happiness. In recovery, cultivating a healthy mental landscape supports our progress.

ENHANCING THOUGHT QUALITY

Monitor Your Thoughts: Be mindful of negative thought patterns that arise.

Practice Positive Affirmations: Replace negative thoughts with empowering statements.

Surround Yourself with Positivity: Engage with uplifting people and environments.

My thoughts are positive and empowering. They shape my happiness and well-being.

DAY 317

"When we are no longer able to change a situation, we are challenged to change ourselves." VIKTOR FRANKL

Sometimes, circumstances are beyond our control. In these moments, adapting ourselves is the key to overcoming adversity. From such transformations in recovery, personal growth often arises.

EMBRACING PERSONAL CHANGE

Identify Immutable Situations: Recognize aspects of your life that you cannot alter.

Seek Personal Growth: Determine how you can adjust your attitudes or behaviors in response.

Implement Changes: Take proactive steps to evolve and adapt.

I embrace change within myself. Adaptation leads me to growth and resilience.

DAY 318

"He who laughs at himself never runs out of things to laugh at." EPICTETUS

Today's quote reminds us that embracing humor about ourselves lightens our spirit and fosters resilience. It allows us to navigate life's imperfections with grace. In recovery, this perspective can alleviate stress and promote well-being.

FINDING JOY IN MISTAKES

Recall a Humorous Moment: Think of a time you laughed at yourself and how it felt.

Share a Laugh: Tell a funny story about yourself to a friend or a loved one.

Embrace Imperfections: Accept that making mistakes is human and that they can be a source of joy.

I find joy in my silliness. Mistakes are a part of being human and laughter brings me lightness and ease.

DAY 319

"You become what you give your attention to."
EPICTETUS

Our focus shapes our reality. By directing our attention toward positive pursuits, we cultivate growth in those areas. In recovery, being mindful of where we invest our energy is crucial for progress.

DIRECTING YOUR ATTENTION TO YOUR GOALS

Assess Your Focus: Reflect on what you've been directing most of your attention toward.

Set Intentional Priorities: Decide what areas deserve more of your focus to support your well-being.

Mindful Engagement: Commit to being fully present in activities that align with your goals.

I focus my attention on what nurtures my growth. My energy creates my reality.

DAY 320

"Do not wish for a life without problems. An easy life results in a judgmental and lazy mind." GYEONGHEO

Challenges stimulate growth and keep our minds active and engaged. Embracing difficulties as part of life's journey enhances our resilience; overcoming obstacles strengthens our character and commitment in our recovery journey.

EMBRACING CHALLENGES

Reframe Problems: View challenges as opportunities for learning and growth.

Stay Active Mentally: Engage in activities that stimulate your mind and encourage problem-solving.

Practice Gratitude: Appreciate the lessons that difficulties have taught you thus far.

I embrace challenges as opportunities. They sharpen my mind and strengthen my spirit.

DAY 321

"He has the most who is most content with the least."
DIOGENES

True richness does not lie in material abundance but in finding satisfaction with what we have. By embracing simplicity and appreciating the essentials, we free ourselves from the endless pursuit of more. In recovery, cultivating contentment helps us focus on inner peace and gratitude.

EMBRACING CONTENTMENT

Simplify Possessions: Consider decluttering your space, keeping only items that serve a purpose or bring joy.

Practice Mindful Appreciation: Take time each day to acknowledge and appreciate the simple things in life.

Limit Desires: Before seeking new acquisitions, reflect on whether they align with your needs or are simply temporary wants.

I find richness in simplicity. Contentment fills my life with peace and joy.

DAY 322

"If you accomplish something good with hard work, the labor passes quickly, but the good endures; if you do something shameful in pursuit of pleasure, the pleasure passes quickly, but the shame endures." SENECA

Anticipating pain or hardship often causes more distress than the event itself. By releasing fear, we alleviate unnecessary suffering and open ourselves to peace and possibility. In recovery, facing fears empowers us to move forward with confidence.

LETTING GO OF FEAR

Identify Fears: Write down what you're afraid of and how these fears impact your life.

Challenge Fearful Thoughts: Examine the likelihood of these fears materializing and consider alternative, positive outcomes.

Take Empowered Action: Choose one fear to confront today, even in a small way, to diminish its power over you.

I release fear and embrace courage. Letting go frees me to live fully.

DAY 323

"Do not let what you cannot do interfere with what you can do." JOHN WOODEN

Focusing on limitations hinders progress, while concentrating on our abilities propels us forward. By acknowledging and leveraging our strengths, we can make meaningful strides in our journey. Emphasizing what we can control fosters empowerment and growth in our recovery.

FOCUSING ON ABILITIES

List Your Strengths: Recognize and write down your talents, skills and positive qualities.

Set Achievable Goals: Establish objectives that align with your strengths and interests.

Take Action Steps: Commit to actions that utilize your abilities, and celebrate your successes along the way.

I focus on what I can do. My abilities drive my progress and success.

DAY 324

"We are what we repeatedly do. Excellence, then, is not an act but a habit." ARISTOTLE

Our daily habits shape our character and destiny. By cultivating positive routines, we lay the groundwork for excellence and achievement. In recovery, establishing healthy habits supports a lasting transformation and well-being.

BUILDING POSITIVE HABITS

Identify Key Habits: Choose one habit that will have a significant positive impact on your life.

Create a Plan: Outline the steps to integrate this habit into your daily routine.

Stay Consistent: Monitor your progress and remain committed, adjusting your plan as needed to maintain the habit.

I build excellence through my habits. Consistent actions shape my success.

DAY 325

"He who knows that enough is enough will always have enough." LAO TZU

Recognizing when we have enough brings peace and contentment. By appreciating sufficiency, we free ourselves from the constant desire for more. In recovery as well, this mindset fosters gratitude and satisfaction with the present moment.

RECOGNIZING SUFFICIENCY

Assess Your Needs: Reflect on what truly fulfills you versus fleeting desires.

Practice Mindful Consumption: Before acquiring something new, consider if it aligns with your genuine needs.

Cultivate Gratitude: Regularly acknowledge and appreciate what you already have.

I have enough, and I am enough. Contentment brings me peace and fulfillment.

DAY 326

"The only way to do great work is to love what you do."
STEVE JOBS

Passion fuels excellence and fulfillment. Engaging in activities we love inspires us to reach higher and find joy in our efforts. In recovery, discovering and pursuing our passions enriches our journey and well-being.

PURSUING PASSION

Identify Your Interests: Reflect on activities that bring you joy and excitement.

Integrate Them Daily: Find ways to incorporate these passions into your routine.

Set Passionate Goals: Align your objectives with what you love to enhance motivation and satisfaction.

I engage in what I love. Passion drives my inner fulfillment.

DAY 327

"The true man is revealed in difficult times. So, when trouble comes, think of yourself as a wrestler whom God, like a trainer, has paired with a tough young buck." EPICTETUS

Both achievements and setbacks are temporary. What truly matters is our determination to keep moving forward. In recovery, resilience and perseverance are essential for sustained progress.

BUILDING PERSEVERANCE

Embrace Both Highs and Lows: View both successes and failures as part of the growth process.

Maintain Determination: Reaffirm your commitment to your recovery journey daily.

Seek Support: Connect with others who can encourage and support you during challenging times.

I persist with courage. Continuing forward defines my strength and character.

DAY 328

"It always seems impossible until it's done."
NELSON MANDELA

Tasks may appear daunting until we accomplish them. Believing in our ability to overcome challenges propels us toward success, and it is crucial to have faith in ourselves and our recovery process.

BELIEVING IN POSSIBILITY

Recall Past Triumphs: Remember times when you achieved what once seemed impossible.

Set Ambitious Goals: Challenge yourself with objectives that inspire growth.

Visualize Achievement: Regularly imagine yourself reaching your goals to reinforce belief.

I believe in possibilities. What seems impossible becomes achievable through effort and determination.

DAY 329

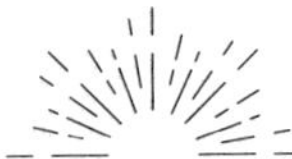

"Whoever is happy will make others happy too."
ANNE FRANK

Happiness brings people together and fosters healthy relationships. By sharing warmth and kindness, we contribute to a more peaceful world. In our recovery journey too, small acts of goodwill enhance our own happiness and that of others.

SPREADING POSITIVITY

Smile Intentionally: Make a conscious effort to smile at people you encounter today.

Offer Kind Words: Compliment or express appreciation for someone.

Reflect on the Impact: Notice how these actions affect your mood and the responses of others.

I spread peace with simple acts. My smile brings joy to myself and those around me.

DAY 330

"It takes courage to grow up and become who you really are." E.E. CUMMINGS

Embracing our unique journey allows us to live authentically and make meaningful contributions. By forging our own path, we also inspire others and create a legacy. In recovery, honoring our individuality empowers us to not only overcome challenges, but achieve personal fulfilment as well.

EMBRACING INDIVIDUALITY

Acknowledge Your Uniqueness: Reflect on the qualities and experiences that make you who you are.

Pursue Personal Goals: Focus on aspirations that resonate with your true self, regardless of others' expectations.

Inspire Others: Share your journey and encourage others to embrace their own paths.

I create my own path with courage and authenticity. My unique journey leaves a meaningful trail.

DAY 331

"Be kind whenever possible. It is always possible."
DALAI LAMA

Kindness is a powerful force that can transform our interactions and the world around us. By choosing to be kind even in challenging situations, we uplift ourselves and others. In recovery, practicing kindness fosters empathy and strengthens our relationships.

CULTIVATING KINDNESS

Act with Compassion: Perform an act of kindness today, no matter how small.

Practice Empathy: Try to understand others' perspectives and feelings.

Reflect on Kindness Received: Recall times when someone else's kindness impacted you and how it made you feel.

I choose kindness in all my interactions. My compassion enriches my life and those around me.

DAY 332

"Be yourself—not your idea of what you think somebody else's idea of yourself should be."
HENRY DAVID THOREAU

Authenticity requires courage to live in alignment with our highest values and truths. When we act according to our inner wisdom, we honor ourselves and our journey. So, in recovery, being true to ourselves strengthens our resolve and integrity.

EMBRACING AUTHENTICITY

Identify Core Values: Reflect on your most important principles.

Align Actions: Ensure that your decisions and behaviors reflect these values.

Express Your Truth: Share your thoughts and feelings honestly and respectfully.

I live authentically, honoring my true self. Integrity guides my path.

DAY 333

"The past cannot be changed. The future is yet in your power." MARY PICKFORD

Dwelling on past mistakes hinders our ability to move forward. While we cannot alter what has passed, we have the power to shape our future through the choices we make today. In recovery as well, focusing on the present empowers us to create a better tomorrow.

LETTING GO OF THE PAST

Acknowledge Past Lessons: Recognize what you've learned from previous experiences.

Release Regrets: Practice forgiveness toward yourself and others.

Set Future Goals: Define positive actions you can take moving forward.

I release the past and embrace the future. My choices today shape my tomorrow.

DAY 334

"The mind is not a vessel to be filled but a fire to be kindled." PLUTARCH

Today's quote emphasizes that education and growth are not just about absorbing information but igniting curiosity and passion within ourselves. In recovery as well, nurturing our interests and seeking knowledge invigorates our spirit and supports personal development.

IGNITING YOUR MIND

Pursue Learning: Engage with a topic or skill that excites you.

Ask Questions: Cultivate curiosity by exploring new ideas.

Share Knowledge: Discuss your interests with others to deepen understanding.

I kindle the fire of my mind. Curiosity and learning enrich my life.

DAY 335

"Everything turns on your assumptions about it, and that's on you. You can pluck out the hasty judgment at will." MARCUS AURELIUS

With today's quote, Marcus Aurelius enforces that assumptions, judgments and doubts can be barriers to achieving our goals and dreams, but by believing in ourselves and our potential, we unlock possibilities for the future. In recovery, overcoming self-doubt is crucial for progress and transformation.

OVERCOMING DOUBT AND DISTRESSING THOUGHTS

Identify Limiting Beliefs: Write down doubts that hold you back.

Challenge These Beliefs: Replace them with positive affirmations and evidence of your capabilities.

Take Confident Action: Do something today that reinforces your self-belief.

I release doubt and embrace confidence. My belief in myself shapes my reality.

DAY 336

"The journey, not the destination, matters." T.S. ELIOT

While goals are important, it's the experiences and growth along the way that truly enrich our lives. In recovery, embracing the process allows us to appreciate each step and the lessons it brings.

EMBRACING THE JOURNEY

Be Present: Focus on the experiences of today rather than fixating on outcomes.

Celebrate Small Wins: Acknowledge and appreciate progress, no matter how minor.

Reflect on Growth: Consider how far you've come since beginning your journey.

I cherish each moment of my journey. Growth unfolds with every step.

DAY 337

Waiting passively rarely leads to improvement because positive change requires intentional action. In recovery, proactively making changes empowers us to create the life we desire.

COMMENCING POSITIVE CHANGE

Identify Areas for Improvement: Reflect on aspects of your life you'd like to enhance.

Set Actionable Steps: Develop a plan to implement changes.

Commit to Action: Begin today, taking the first step toward transformation.

I create positive change in my life. My actions lead to improvement and growth.

DAY 338

"'Hope' is the thing with feathers that perches in the soul." EMILY DICKINSON

Today's quote reminds us that hope inspires us to persevere through challenges and believe in better days ahead. It fuels resilience and optimism. In our recovery journey too, nurturing hope strengthens our resolve and uplifts our spirit.

CULTIVATING HOPE

Visualize Positive Outcomes: Spend some time imagining a successful and fulfilling future for yourself.

Seek Inspiration: Read stories or quotes that uplift and encourage you.

Share Hope: Offer words of encouragement to someone who may need it.

Hope fills my soul and guides me forward. I believe in a brighter tomorrow.

DAY 339

"In the middle of difficulty lies opportunity."
ANONYMOUS

Challenges often present hidden opportunities for growth and learning. By shifting our perspective, we can uncover potential benefits within hardships. In recovery, viewing difficulties as opportunities empowers us to adapt and evolve.

FINDING OPPORTUNITIES IN CHALLENGES

Reframe Difficulties: Identify a current challenge and consider what opportunities it might offer.

Set Growth Goals: Determine how you can use this challenge to develop new skills or strengths.

Take Proactive Steps: Act on the opportunities identified to turn adversity into advantage.

I find opportunities within challenges. Difficulties become stepping stones to growth.

DAY 340

"Happiness is not by chance but by choice."
JIM ROHN

Happiness results from intentional decisions rather than external circumstances. By choosing attitudes and actions that align with our joy and contentment, we shape our own well-being. In recovery too, making conscious choices supports a fulfilling life.

CHOOSING HAPPINESS

Practice Gratitude: Begin your day by acknowledging things you're thankful for.

Engage in Joyful Activities: Dedicate time to pursuits that bring you genuine happiness.

Cultivate Positive Relationships: Surround yourself with people who uplift and support you.

I choose happiness in my life. My decisions foster joy and fulfillment.

DAY 341

"Everyone thinks of changing the world, but no one thinks of changing himself." LEO TOLSTOY

Before expecting things to change in our favor, we must strive to make changes within ourselves. Once we are on the path to recovery, we become the example by which we lead and inspire change in others. In recovery, by working to embody the qualities we value, we influence our environment positively.

INSPIRING CHANGE IN OURSELVES AND OTHERS

Identify Desired Traits: Reflect on the qualities you admire and wish to cultivate.

Incorporate These Traits: Practice actions today that reflect these qualities.

Inspire Others: Share your experiences to motivate those around you.

I am the change I want to see. My actions inspire transformation in myself and others.

DAY 342

"The secret of change is to focus all of your energy not on fighting the old but on building the new."
SOCRATES

Accepting that change is inevitable allows us to adapt and grow. In our recovery journey as well, embracing change helps us navigate new challenges and opportunities with resilience.

EMBRACING CHANGE

Acknowledge Change: Reflect on recent changes in your life and how they've impacted you.

Adapt Positively: Find ways to adjust your mindset to accommodate these changes.

Seek Growth: View changes as opportunities for personal development.

I embrace change as a natural part of life. Adaptability strengthens me.

DAY 343

"Everything should be made as simple as possible, but not simpler." ALBERT EINSTEIN

The above quote by Einstein reinforces that by focusing on what truly matters, we reduce stress and enhance our well-being; that simplifying our lives brings clarity and peace. In recovery, simplicity helps us maintain our focus on our goals.

SIMPLIFYING YOUR LIFE

Declutter Space: Organize your environment to remove unnecessary items.

Simplify Schedule: Prioritize activities that align with your values and eliminate excess commitments.

Mindful Consumption: Be intentional about what you bring into your life.

I find peace in simplicity. Letting go of excess brings clarity to my life.

DAY 344

"He who knows himself is enlightened." LAO TZU

Self-awareness is the foundation of personal growth. By knowing our thoughts and emotions, we make informed choices that align with our true selves. In recovery, self-knowledge empowers us in overcoming challenges.

DEEPENING SELF-AWARENESS

Self-Reflection: Spend time journaling about your feelings and behaviors.

Identify Patterns: Notice recurring thoughts or actions that may need adjustment.

Seek Insight: Consider feedback from trusted friends or mentors.

I seek to know myself deeply. Self-awareness guides my growth.

DAY 345

"Act without expectation." LAO TZU

Engaging in actions without attachment to outcomes allows us to experience life more fully. In recovery, focusing on the process rather than the result reduces anxiety and fosters contentment.

PRACTICING DETACHMENT

Mindful Actions: Engage in tasks wholeheartedly without fixating on the end result.

Release Expectations: Let go of desires to achieve specific outcomes and remain open to possibilities.

Reflect on Experience: Focus on what you learn and how you grow from each action.

I act with purpose but without expectation. Freedom comes from releasing attachment.

DAY 346

"From caring comes courage." LAO TZU

Compassion for ourselves and others fuels bravery. When we care deeply, we find the strength to face challenges, and in recovery, nurturing kindness bolsters our resilience as well.

CULTIVATING COMPASSION

Self-Care: Engage in activities that promote your well-being.

Extend Kindness: Perform an act of kindness for someone else.

Empathize: Try to understand others' feelings and perspectives.

My compassion gives me courage. Caring strengthens my spirit.

DAY 347

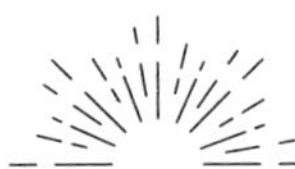

"Wherever you go, go with all your heart."
CONFUCIUS

By engaging in anything wholeheartedly, we find deeper meaning and satisfaction, as fully committing to our endeavors enriches our experiences. In recovery, wholeheartedness supports a lasting change.

POSITIVE ENGAGEMENT

Be Present: Completely focus your attention on the task at hand.

Align with Passion: Pursue activities that resonate with your values and interests.

Reflect on Commitment: Consider how giving your all enhances your experiences.

I engage fully in all I do. My sincerity brings me fulfillment.

DAY 348

"The best way out is always through." ROBERT FROST

Today's quote by Robert Frost reminds us that facing challenges bravely leads to resolution and growth. Avoiding difficulties often prolongs discomfort, and in recovery, confronting issues head-on promotes healing.

FACING CHALLENGES

Identify Avoidances: Recognize any problems you've been hesitant to address.

Develop a Plan: Outline steps to confront these issues constructively.

Take Action: Begin by tackling one challenge today.

I face challenges directly. Moving through them leads to growth.

DAY 349

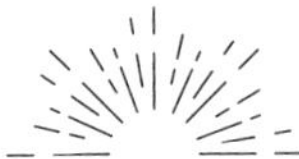

"This too shall pass." PERSIAN PROVERB

Remembering that all situations are temporary helps us maintain perspective. In difficult times, it offers hope; in good times, it fosters gratitude. In recovery, this awareness supports emotional balance.

EMBRACING TRANSIENCY

Mindfulness Practice: Stay present and appreciate the current moment.

Perspective Taking: In tough times, remind yourself that the situation is temporary.

Gratitude Expression: Cherish positive experiences knowing they are fleeting.

I accept the impermanence of life. Understanding this brings me peace.

DAY 350

"Do small things with great love." MOTHER TERESA

Acts of love and kindness, no matter how small, make a significant impact. By infusing our actions with care, we contribute positively to the world. In our own recovery journey too, this practice nurtures our spirit and those of others.

ACTING WITH LOVE

Mindful Kindness: Perform a simple act of kindness today.

Attention to Detail: Approach tasks with care and consideration.

Share Gratitude: Express your appreciation for someone who has helped you.

I bring love to everything I do. Small acts make a big difference.

DAY 351

"The only true wisdom is in knowing you know nothing."
SOCRATES

Admitting that we don't have all the answers opens us up to learning and growth. In recovery, humility allows us to remain teachable and receptive to new insights that can aid our journey.

EMBRACING HUMILITY

Acknowledge Limitations: Reflect on areas where you can learn more.

Seek Knowledge: Engage with books, mentors or support groups to expand your understanding.

Practice Open-Mindedness: Be willing to consider new perspectives and ideas.

I embrace humility. Being open allows me to grow and learn each day.

DAY 352

"How satisfying it is to dismiss and block out any upsetting or foreign impression, and immediately to have peace in all things." MARCUS AURELIUS

Holding on to resentment only harms us; so, instead of seeking retaliation, we can choose to act with integrity and kindness. In recovery, letting go of grudges frees us to focus on our own healing.

LEAVING RESENTMENT

Identify Grudges: Acknowledge any lingering resentments you may hold.

Practice Forgiveness: Release the desire for revenge, understanding that it benefits your well-being.

Choose Positive Actions: Respond to negativity with compassion or by setting healthy boundaries.

I release resentment and embrace forgiveness. My peace is more important than holding on to anger.

DAY 353

"You have power over your mind—not outside events. Realize this, and you will find strength."
MARCUS AURELIUS

Focusing on what we can control—our thoughts and reactions—truly empowers us, while accepting that external events are often beyond our control reduces frustration and anxiety. In recovery, this internal focus supports emotional stability and resilience.

CULTIVATING CONTROL

Mindful Awareness: Observe your thoughts and feelings without judgment.

Practice Response over Reaction: Instead of reacting impulsively to triggers, pause to carefully consider how you should react to the situation.

Set Intentions: Begin each day with a positive affirmation or goal to guide your mindset.

I control my thoughts and reactions. My inner strength guides me through life's challenges.

DAY 354

"Waste no more time arguing what a good man should be. Be one." MARCUS AURELIUS

Rather than debating virtues, embody them through your actions. In recovery, living out our values speaks louder than words and inspires others by example.

EMBODYING YOUR VALUES

Define Your Virtues: Identify the qualities you wish to embody, such as honesty, courage or kindness.

Act Accordingly: Make conscious choices that reflect these virtues in your daily life.

Reflect on Actions: At the end of the day, consider how your actions aligned with your values and where you can improve.

I live my values through my actions. Being the person I aspire to be brings me fulfillment.

DAY 355

"The happiness of your life depends upon the quality of your thoughts." MARCUS AURELIUS

Our mindset profoundly affects our experience of life, and nurturing positive and constructive thoughts enhances our well-being. In recovery, cultivating a healthy mental landscape supports our healing journey as well.

NURTURING POSITIVE THOUGHTS

Monitor Inner Dialogue: Be aware of negative self-talk and challenge unhelpful thoughts.

Practice Gratitude: Focus on what you are thankful for to foster a positive outlook.

Affirmations: Use positive statements to reinforce self-belief and optimism.

My thoughts shape my reality. I choose to think positively and cultivate happiness.

DAY 356

"If you are distressed by anything external, the pain is not due to the thing itself but to your estimate of it."
MARCUS AURELIUS

Our perceptions determine how we experience events. By reframing our thoughts, we can reduce distress and find peace. In recovery, adjusting our mindset helps us navigate challenges more effectively.

REFRAMING PERSPECTIVES

Identify Distressing Thoughts: Notice situations that cause you discomfort.

Challenge Your Interpretation: Ask yourself if there is another way to view the situation.

Choose a Constructive Perspective: Focus on what you can learn or how you can grow from the experience.

I have the power to change my perspective. I choose thoughts that bring me peace.

DAY 357

"If you want something good, get it from yourself."
EPICTETUS

Clarity about who we want to become guides our actions. By setting a vision for ourselves, we can align our efforts accordingly. In recovery, this intentionality fosters purposeful growth.

DEFINING YOUR VISION

Visualize Your Best Self: Describe the person you aspire to be in detail. What virtues or qualities do you possess in this vision?

Set Aligned Goals: Create objectives that support this vision.

Take Consistent Action: Implement daily habits that move you toward your desired self.

I know who I want to be and take steps each day to become that person.

DAY 358

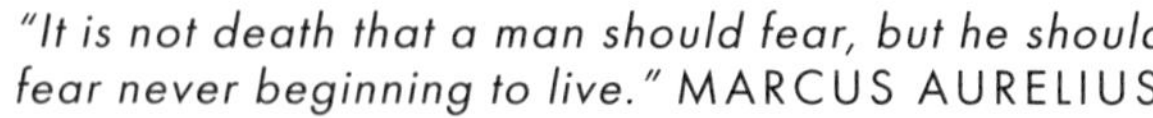
"It is not death that a man should fear, but he should fear never beginning to live." MARCUS AURELIUS

Marcus Aurelius, with today's quote, reminds us that true loss is not in dying but in failing to truly live. Embracing life fully allows us to experience joy, love and fulfillment. In recovery, stepping into life with enthusiasm enriches our journey.

EMBRACING LIFE FULLY

Engage in Meaningful Activities: Pursue passions and interests that bring you joy.

Connect with Others: Build and nurture relationships that add value to your life.

Practice Mindfulness: Be present in each moment, appreciating life's experiences.

I embrace life fully. Living authentically brings me joy and fulfillment.

DAY 359

"Do what you can, with what you have, where you are."
THEODORE ROOSEVELT

We may not have perfect circumstances, but we can make the most of what we have. In recovery, taking action within our current situation propels us forward and fosters empowerment.

MAXIMIZING THE PRESENT

Assess Your Resources: Identify the tools, support and abilities you currently possess.

Set Realistic Goals: Focus on achievable steps you can take now with the resources you have.

Take Initiative: Begin today to make progress.

I have enough to make the most of the present moment. My actions today create a better tomorrow.

DAY 360

"If anyone can refute me—show me I'm making a mistake or looking at things from the wrong perspective—I'll gladly change. It's the truth I'm after, and the truth never harmed anyone." MARCUS AURELIUS

This quote reflects an openness to changing beliefs based on new insights. Growth requires adaptability and a willingness to evolve. Embracing change allows us to continually refine ourselves, and in recovery, being open to change fosters ongoing improvement and self-discovery.

EMBRACING CONTINUOUS IMPROVEMENT

Welcome Feedback: Be open to constructive criticism and new ideas. Purposely seek out people who can introduce you to new perspectives.

Adapt and Adjust: Be willing to alter habits or strategies that no longer serve you.

Commit to Lifelong Learning: Seek opportunities to expand your knowledge and skills.

I embrace change as a pathway to growth. Continual improvement improves my life.

DAY 361

"The obstacle is the way." MARCUS AURELIUS

Challenges are not roadblocks but essential parts of our journey. By embracing obstacles, we transform them into opportunities for growth. In recovery, viewing difficulties as pathways helps us stay motivated and resilient.

EMBRACING OBSTACLES

Identify Current Challenges: List the obstacles you're facing in your recovery journey.

Reframe the Situation: Consider what each obstacle is teaching you about yourself.

Take Constructive Action: Develop a plan to address these challenges positively.

I embrace obstacles as opportunities. Each challenge strengthens me and guides my growth.

DAY 362

"Knowing yourself is the beginning of all wisdom."
ARISTOTLE

Self-knowledge is the foundation for making wise choices. Understanding our thoughts, emotions and patterns allows us to navigate life with greater clarity. In our recovery journey as well, self-awareness empowers us to heal and grow intentionally.

DEEPENING KNOWLEDGE

Self-Reflection: Take time to explore your emotions, reactions and desires.

Track Your Patterns: Note recurring behaviors or thoughts that may need adjustment.

Seek External Insight: Engage with a trusted friend or therapist for further perspective.

I know myself deeply. Wisdom comes from understanding my true self.

DAY 363

"He who reigns within himself and rules passions, desires and fears is more than a king." JOHN MILTON

While emotions and circumstances come and go like weather patterns, our true essence is constant and unchanging. In recovery, recognizing this distinction allows us to remain grounded even in times of turmoil.

CULTIVATING STABILITY

Identify Temporary Emotions: Reflect on emotions that pass like weather rather than define you.

Focus on Inner Strength: Visualize your core self as steady and unaffected by temporary setbacks.

Let Go of Attachments: Cease defining your identity by the fleeting moods or situations you experience.

I am grounded in my true self. Emotions and circumstances pass, but I remain steady.

DAY 364

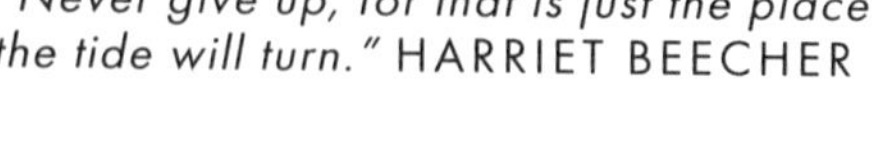

"Never give up, for that is just the place and time that the tide will turn." HARRIET BEECHER STOWE

Setbacks are a natural part of life; what matters is how we respond to them. Each time we rise after a fall, we strengthen our resilience and perseverance. In recovery, bouncing back from challenges builds character and determination.

BUILDING RESILIENCE

Reflect on Past Recoveries: Recall times when you were tempted to give up but chose to overcome the challenge. Note how you managed to rise.

Develop Coping Strategies: Identify tools and support systems that help you bounce back from setbacks.

Embrace the Lesson: View every setback as an opportunity to learn and grow.

I rise stronger each time I fall. Resilience carries me through life's ups and downs.

DAY 365

"The journey of a thousand miles begins with one step."
LAO TZU

Every great achievement starts with small, consistent actions. By focusing on one step at a time, we build momentum and move closer to our goals. In our recovery journey as well, daily effort and perseverance are keys to lasting success.

TAKING SMALL STEPS

Set a Small Goal: Identify one action you can take today toward your long-term recovery.

Focus on the Present Moment: Instead of worrying about the entire journey, concentrate on the step before you.

Celebrate Progress: Acknowledge the significance of each small step taken and how far you've come.

I move forward one step at a time. Each action brings me closer to my goals.

BEGIN AGAIN

This section is for the days you missed journaling. These pages offer space to pause, return and move forward. Begin again with presence and control.

"Every new beginning comes from some other beginning's end." SENECA

YOU'VE RETURNED. THAT'S ALL THAT MATTERS.

Use this space to reflect, reset or simply reconnect with your path.

➼ *What do I need to leave behind today?*

➼ *What do I want to carry forward?*

➼ *What's one thing I can do right now to feel aligned with my values?*

I begin again—not from scratch but with strength.

"As long as you live, keep learning how to live."
SENECA

YOU'VE RETURNED. THAT'S ALL THAT MATTERS.

Use this space to reflect, reset or simply reconnect with your path.

➸ *What do I need to leave behind today?*

➸ *What do I want to carry forward?*

➸ *What's one thing I can do right now to feel aligned with my values?*

I do not begin at zero. I begin with experience.

"Every new beginning comes from some other beginning's end." SENECA

YOU'VE RETURNED. THAT'S ALL THAT MATTERS.

Use this space to reflect, reset or simply reconnect with your path.

➼ *What do I need to leave behind today?*

➼ *What do I want to carry forward?*

➼ *What's one thing I can do right now to feel aligned with my values?*

I begin again—not from scratch but with strength.

"As long as you live, keep learning how to live."
SENECA

YOU'VE RETURNED. THAT'S ALL THAT MATTERS.

Use this space to reflect, reset or simply reconnect with your path.

➵ *What do I need to leave behind today?*

➵ *What do I want to carry forward?*

➵ *What's one thing I can do right now to feel aligned with my values?*

I do not begin at zero. I begin with experience.

"Every new beginning comes from some other beginning's end." SENECA

YOU'VE RETURNED. THAT'S ALL THAT MATTERS.

Use this space to reflect, reset or simply reconnect with your path.

➻ *What do I need to leave behind today?*

➻ *What do I want to carry forward?*

➻ *What's one thing I can do right now to feel aligned with my values?*

I begin again—not from scratch but with strength.

"As long as you live, keep learning how to live."
SENECA

YOU'VE RETURNED. THAT'S ALL THAT MATTERS.

Use this space to reflect, reset or simply reconnect with your path.

➵ *What do I need to leave behind today?*

➵ *What do I want to carry forward?*

➵ *What's one thing I can do right now to feel aligned with my values?*

I do not begin at zero. I begin with experience.

"Every new beginning comes from some other beginning's end." SENECA

YOU'VE RETURNED. THAT'S ALL THAT MATTERS.

Use this space to reflect, reset or simply reconnect with your path.

➵ *What do I need to leave behind today?*

➵ *What do I want to carry forward?*

➵ *What's one thing I can do right now to feel aligned with my values?*

I begin again—not from scratch but with strength.

"As long as you live, keep learning how to live."
SENECA

YOU'VE RETURNED. THAT'S ALL THAT MATTERS.

Use this space to reflect, reset or simply reconnect with your path.

➺ *What do I need to leave behind today?*

➺ *What do I want to carry forward?*

➺ *What's one thing I can do right now to feel aligned with my values?*

I do not begin at zero. I begin with experience.

"Every new beginning comes from some other beginning's end." SENECA

YOU'VE RETURNED. THAT'S ALL THAT MATTERS.

Use this space to reflect, reset or simply reconnect with your path.

➼ *What do I need to leave behind today?*

➼ *What do I want to carry forward?*

➼ *What's one thing I can do right now to feel aligned with my values?*

I begin again—not from scratch but with strength.

"As long as you live, keep learning how to live."
SENECA

YOU'VE RETURNED. THAT'S ALL THAT MATTERS.

Use this space to reflect, reset or simply reconnect with your path.

➵ *What do I need to leave behind today?*

➵ *What do I want to carry forward?*

➵ *What's one thing I can do right now to feel aligned with my values?*

I do not begin at zero. I begin with experience.

"Every new beginning comes from some other beginning's end." SENECA

YOU'VE RETURNED. THAT'S ALL THAT MATTERS.

Use this space to reflect, reset or simply reconnect with your path.

➾ *What do I need to leave behind today?*

➾ *What do I want to carry forward?*

➾ *What's one thing I can do right now to feel aligned with my values?*

I begin again—not from scratch but with strength.

"As long as you live, keep learning how to live."
SENECA

YOU'VE RETURNED. THAT'S ALL THAT MATTERS.

Use this space to reflect, reset or simply reconnect with your path.

➵ *What do I need to leave behind today?*

➵ *What do I want to carry forward?*

➵ *What's one thing I can do right now to feel aligned with my values?*

I do not begin at zero. I begin with experience.

"Every new beginning comes from some other beginning's end." SENECA

YOU'VE RETURNED. THAT'S ALL THAT MATTERS.

Use this space to reflect, reset or simply reconnect with your path.

➸ *What do I need to leave behind today?*

➸ *What do I want to carry forward?*

➸ *What's one thing I can do right now to feel aligned with my values?*

I begin again—not from scratch but with strength.

"As long as you live, keep learning how to live."
SENECA

YOU'VE RETURNED. THAT'S ALL THAT MATTERS.

Use this space to reflect, reset or simply reconnect with your path.

➵ *What do I need to leave behind today?*

➵ *What do I want to carry forward?*

➵ *What's one thing I can do right now to feel aligned with my values?*

I do not begin at zero. I begin with experience.

"Every new beginning comes from some other beginning's end." SENECA

YOU'VE RETURNED. THAT'S ALL THAT MATTERS.

Use this space to reflect, reset or simply reconnect with your path.

➼ *What do I need to leave behind today?*

➼ *What do I want to carry forward?*

➼ *What's one thing I can do right now to feel aligned with my values?*

I begin again—not from scratch but with strength.

"As long as you live, keep learning how to live."
SENECA

YOU'VE RETURNED. THAT'S ALL THAT MATTERS.

Use this space to reflect, reset or simply reconnect with your path.

➵ *What do I need to leave behind today?*

➵ *What do I want to carry forward?*

➵ *What's one thing I can do right now to feel aligned with my values?*

I do not begin at zero. I begin with experience.

"Every new beginning comes from some other beginning's end." SENECA

YOU'VE RETURNED. THAT'S ALL THAT MATTERS.

Use this space to reflect, reset or simply reconnect with your path.

➼ *What do I need to leave behind today?*

➼ *What do I want to carry forward?*

➼ *What's one thing I can do right now to feel aligned with my values?*

I begin again—not from scratch but with strength.

"As long as you live, keep learning how to live."
SENECA

YOU'VE RETURNED. THAT'S ALL THAT MATTERS.

Use this space to reflect, reset or simply reconnect with your path.

➛ *What do I need to leave behind today?*

➛ *What do I want to carry forward?*

➛ *What's one thing I can do right now to feel aligned with my values?*

I do not begin at zero. I begin with experience.

"Every new beginning comes from some other beginning's end." SENECA

YOU'VE RETURNED. THAT'S ALL THAT MATTERS.

Use this space to reflect, reset or simply reconnect with your path.

➸ *What do I need to leave behind today?*

➸ *What do I want to carry forward?*

➸ *What's one thing I can do right now to feel aligned with my values?*

I begin again—not from scratch but with strength.

"As long as you live, keep learning how to live."
SENECA

YOU'VE RETURNED. THAT'S ALL THAT MATTERS.

Use this space to reflect, reset or simply reconnect with your path.

➵ *What do I need to leave behind today?*

➵ *What do I want to carry forward?*

➵ *What's one thing I can do right now to feel aligned with my values?*

I do not begin at zero. I begin with experience.

"Every new beginning comes from some other beginning's end." SENECA

YOU'VE RETURNED. THAT'S ALL THAT MATTERS.

Use this space to reflect, reset or simply reconnect with your path.

➵ *What do I need to leave behind today?*

➵ *What do I want to carry forward?*

➵ *What's one thing I can do right now to feel aligned with my values?*

I begin again—not from scratch but with strength.